The 13th Sign

The Zodiac Has Changed, So Have You: Find Out How and Why.

By

Mary Francis Abbamonte

ISBN: 0-7596-8056-6

This book is printed on acid free paper.

Cover: The background is – The 13th Sign – Ophiuchus, that contains some of the most colorful and spectacular nebulae ever photographed. © Anglo-Australian Observatory, Photograph from UK Schmidt plates by David Malin.

1stBooks - rev. 05/16/02

This book is dedicated to:

Paul Breidbord who believed in me and gave the encouragement I needed to complete this book.

My son Joseph Toto.

My friends Carl and Bonnie Takakjian.

My Monday night meditation group.

My dear old friend Suellen Rubinstein, who magically showed up, just when I needed some wisdom and words.

&

To all my fellow travelers seeking a higher purpose and a better understanding of their journey in life.

TABLE OF CONTENTS

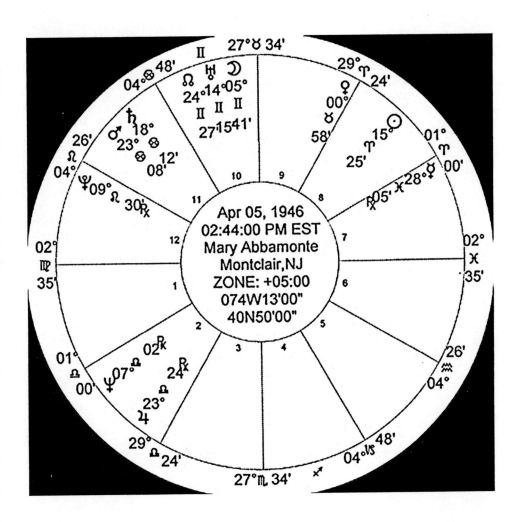

FOREWORD

Astrology is astronomy brought to Earth and applied to the affairs of men.
—Ralph Waldo Emerson (1803-82)

To readers who are astrologers, I was born April 5, 1946 in Montclair, New Jersey at 2:44 p.m. and presently living in Stamford, Connecticut (see birth/natal chart page ix)

To readers who are not astrologers, this is what an astrological birth/natal chart looks like.

From this chart, the astrologer can know more about me—and whether or not I am good at what I do—than my closest friends or family members. But since not all of you are astrologers yet, here are a few words about my background and how I got started with astrology.

In the late sixties, the glory days of advertising, I was living in New York City, working as a fashion designer and stylist for professional photographers. I was also going to numerous parties and Broadway plays. I first heard the song "This is the dawning of the Age of Aquarius" at the opening performance of "Hair" at the Biltmore theater on Broadway. The song went on, "When the moon is in the Seventh House/ And Jupiter aligns with Mars/Then peace will guide the planets/And love will steer the stars." I had to know more.

At that time, the United States was torn apart by the Vietnam War and Woodstock hadn't happened yet. That is where my personal journey began. I started reading everything I could find on astrology. Back then, prior to the widespread use of computers, it took days of mathematical computations and calculations to set up a basic natal/birth chart before you could even begin to figure out what the chart meant. Today, with computer software designed for such astrological calculations, it only takes seconds to do a chart. However, the interpretations of astrology are a life-long study.

Soon after seeing "Hair," I started working with astrology at night. I then began doing charts in studios and on film sets for actors and directors. In 1989, I became a full time astrologist. I am still a member of the United Scenic Artists Union and New York Women in Film. I am also a member of the Association for Astrological Networking (AFAM), the American

Federation of Astrologers (AFA), and the International Society for Astrological Research (ISAR). I am an Intuitive Constant and have a private practice in the New York metropolitan area. I also give workshops and teach astrology and tarot in Greenwich, Connecticut, and I appear on local cable television shows as an astrologist.

But who am I? I am still that pure spirit (we all begin life as pure spirits) who grew up in a large family in New Jersey. My father was a country doctor who delivered most of the babies in town and made house calls in the middle of the night. He believed that taking care of the whole body was important-so important that he founded the committee on medicine and religion at the Essex County Medical Society in New Jersey. He was also the first doctor to say that there should be a priest, minster or rabbi in every hospital in the state, and he began a campaign to train chaplains to serve also as healers.

"Since about fifty per cent of all illness is emotionally caused," he told a newspaper reporter, "a sympathetic ear is sometimes more healing than medicine." He continued, "A man with a stomach condition may be having difficulties with his wife or his job, but even if there's a real physical disturbance, emotions can make it worse."

A general practitioner or a chaplain who is willing to listen can help tremendously.

He also said that in most cases, a psychiatrist was not the answer, and that specialists were usually too busy to do anything but practice their specialties. "What patients usually need," my father believed, "is a little spiritual or emotional adjustment."

Like my father, I was a bit of a rebel. Unlike him, I had no interest in going to medical school. Plus, I was an undiagnosed dyslexic (in my birth chart, "Mercury Rx" means that Mercury, the "messenger," is in retrograde, the illusion of going backward in the sky. Whenever Mercury is in retrograde, about three times a year, people have problems with communication. For example, a stamp falls off of a letter, or voters get confused in voting booths, as happened in the election in 2000.) As you may know, most dyslexics tend to have unusual or highly creative perceptions and thoughts. Sometimes this leads to new ideas and breakthroughs. Sometimes it makes it hard just to get through grade school.

My mother, a nurse, a Catholic, was of Irish-Scottish descent (the Irish in me might explain my interest in the magical and mystical). She believed that the nuns who taught at the parochial grade school I attended were always right. And, of course, and in those days, few people knew about dyslexia. My small private catholic school in an old mansion in South Orange had angels painted all over the ceilings. School was so difficult for me, and the nuns were so mean, that I would escape into the world of angels.

The high school I went to was also private, and Catholic. This school was huge, bulging with Baby Boomers in classes three times the size of any classes the school had ever experienced before. The school didn't know what to do with all of us—I got lost in the crowd. But I also discovered boys and had great fun. No more talking with the angels-until, that is, my hippie days and Woodstock.

As I've said, I was never interested in medicine or healing. But I was good at art and loved fashion and design. So, at 18, I went off to New York to find my fame and fortune. My love for the world of fashion and photography led to my becoming a fashion stylist. I also married a well-known advertising photographer (now passed over). With him I had a son named Joseph, who is a beautiful person both inside and out. He is the light of my life.

But what, specifically, made me so interested in this 13th Sign, Ophiuchus? Ophiuchus is the god of medicine. I began to read up on alternative medicine in 1985, when my younger sister was battling cancer. It seemed to me that there had to be a reason for all that pain. I read her astrological charts over and over and I saw that she had a choice, as we all do, to change, learn and move on.

Drawing on what my father had said about spirituality many years before, I started my search into the metaphysical. I found that each of us is our own physician. Obviously there are times when we may need professional help, but true healing comes from happiness within. Happiness is not some dusty old word that conjures up nostalgic times, or promises some distant nirvana. Rather, happiness is essential to our health and well-being.

PREFACE
The Basics: A Crash Course in Astrology

Millionaires don't use astrology, billionaires do.
—J.P. Morgan

For those who are not acquainted with astrology, what follows is a five-minute "crash course" in the subject. At the end of this "course," you will know more about astrology than ninety percent of the population. I have used technical terms and some so-called "New Age" jargon, but don't shy away from this. I believe that if you are going to learn something, do it right, but keep it simple. In the back of the book there is a glossary that will help you understand these terms, as well as a suggested reading list and web sites should you wish to learn more.

Astrology boils down to five basic steps:

> **Step One.** Definition of Zodiac Sun Signs: Where astrology came from.
> **Step Two.** The Planets: This is where the action is, these are the players.
> **Step Three.** The Houses: This is where the action takes place.
> **Step Four.** The Aspects: This is the type of action taking place.
> **Step Five.** The 13th Sign: The Evolvement

Step One: Zodiac Sun Sign
(Note: See chart numbers 1,2,3, and 4)

Zodiac. A band across the heavens made up of the 13 major *constellations* that represent the 13 signs. The Zodiac makes a 360-degree around our universe. (See chart 2, page xxi.)

Sun Sign. The 12 traditional signs of the Zodiac are Aries (the Ram), Taurus (the Bull), Gemini (the Twins), Cancer (the Crab), Leo (the Lion), Virgo (the Virgin), Libra (the Scales), Scorpio (the Scorpion), Sagittarius (the Archer), Capricorn (the Goat), Aquarius (the Water Bearer), and Pisces (the Fish). Added to these signs is Ophiuchus (the Snake Handler) for a total of 13 signs. (See chart 3 and 4, pages xxii-xiii and page 93.)

Constellation. A group of stars visible from Earth that form a distinctive pattern and have a name linked to its shape, often derived from Greek mythology. There are 88 constellations covering our sky; 13 of the constellations are in the Zodiac and are called Sun Signs.

Astrology. The study of the position of the Moon, Sun, and other planets in the belief that their motions affect human beings. Astrology appears to have always been with us. Early man looked up at the magnificent stars in the sky and knew they greatly affected his spirit. The sky looked a great deal brighter back then; today electric lights from Earth dim the brilliance of the stars.

While astrology may vary slightly, depending on one's culture, all forms of astrology stem from the same base: A gift passed down from the ancients to be used as a road map to aid you in making clearer choices for a fuller life.

Astrology has always been a product of its historical context. In ancient times, for example, astrology was called the language of the gods. Originally Astrology was thought to be too complex for the common man to fully understand or calculate. In ancient Mesopotamia, astrology was practiced by all; looking upward for guidance was a part of every day life. Many of the tools used in today's astrology date back to Mesopotamia in 6000 B.C. How the ancients developed and used such an elaborate, precise and complex system for forecasting is still a matter of debate among scientists and others (I have my own thoughts that I will go into in Chapter Two).

Over the years Astrology evolved, and the Egyptians, Greeks, and the Celts, contributed their wisdom. The Chinese and the Hindu Vedics took astrology in a slightly different direction; they gave different names and myths to the constellations but it is essentially the same. Then the Europeans and the Church added their own opinions on the subject ("The celestial bodies," wrote Thomas Aquinas in the 13th Century, "are the cause of all that takes place in the sublunar world"). At the same time, across the Atlantic, Native North and South Americans relied on the stars for guidance. Throughout history astrology has been used to counsel kings, rulers, presidents and generals, right up to the present day. (For example: President Reagan and Princes Diana both consulted astrologers. Personally, I also do work with some very high political figures.)

Astronomy. The measurement of the real and apparent movements and the positions of celestial bodies.

Horoscope. An astrological forecast, astrology's description of an individual's personality and future based on the position of the planets in relation to the sign of the zodiac under which the person was born. Also, it is a diagram of planetary relationships, the position of the stars and planets at a particular moment, especially for someone's birth (see chart 1 page ix.) As it is apparent by now, to get a true and accurate reading, there is a lot more involved than reading that cute little paragraph under your birth date in the "Horoscope" section of your newspaper would suggest.

Step Two: The Planets

The planets—Mercury, Venus, Mars, Jupiter Saturn, Uranus, Neptune, Pluto, the Sun and Moon, and sometimes Chiron—are the keys to where the action takes place in your chart (i.e., your individual horoscope). If you are in a city it's hard to see the heavens, but if you are out in the countryside and look up at night, you will see what the ancients saw. The stars that stay still are the constellations; the ones that move are the planets (in ancient times, the word for planet meant, "the wanderer"), roaming into different constellations or signs in the Zodiac, and stirring things up.

Each planet has its own myth, energy, style, personality, agenda, traits, time schedule and reason-or moral to be where it is in the sky at any given time. Similarly, each sign also has its own personality, myth, style, energy and way of reacting.

Like the planets, you have your own individual beliefs, stories, style and energy. When something happens in your life, you react, and you react to different things in different ways at different places and times. The planets, based on your exact birth, time and location, play out these interactions in the sky, depicting what is happening in your life on earth.

Step Three: The Houses (See chart 4, page ix, xxiii and 93.)

All the activity takes place in the 12 houses. Think of it this way: If the "house" is a physical house, the "signs" would the rooms in the house and the planets (wanderers) would then be where the action or energy occurs in that house.

The 12 segments, or houses, of the astrological chart each have their own qualities and influences:

*The first house is the self
*The second house is possessions
*The third house is relationships
*The fourth house is the home
*The fifth house is creativity
*The sixth house is health
*The seventh house is partnership
*The eighth house is needs, sex and death
 Also transformation
*The ninth house is recognition and religion
*The tenth house is one's profession
*The eleventh house is a one's peer
*The twelfth house is mysticism

Step Four: The Aspects

The following terms will be of particular interest to astrologers and advanced students of astrology and are described only briefly here by way of background for general readers.

Aspects are angled *degrees* between planets and houses that form some meaningful combinations; there are 360 degrees in each chart (see chart) Planets have different aspects, the same way that you have different moods. All the planets are at different aspects from each other at different times. They are constantly moving, changing, connecting, or "aspecting," with each other-just as you do with differing people in your life.

Astrology is the art of 'As above, so below,' for what is happening above in the sky is happening below on earth. For example, when you are having a rough day and things seem to be difficult—you may be fighting with everyone, check your chart and you will see that you have a lot of 90-degree angles called *squares*. On the other hand, when you are having a good day and events flow smoothly, check out what the planets are doing. You will probably find all these wonderful 120-degree angles between planets called *trines*.

Step Five: The 13th Sign

As will be described in the following chapter, this "new" sign and its implications for your life is the focus of this book. You can use this information to help you better understand your newspaper horoscope, or you can use this information as a starting point, a catalyst, to study astrology in greater detail. If the latter is the case, in the back on this book I have listed many references and books. There are websites where you can print out your birth or natal chart—your personal blueprint, the road map of your life, based on the date, time and location of your birth; several of these web sites will do your chart free of charge.

Keep an open heart and work with your inner voice.

CHART 2

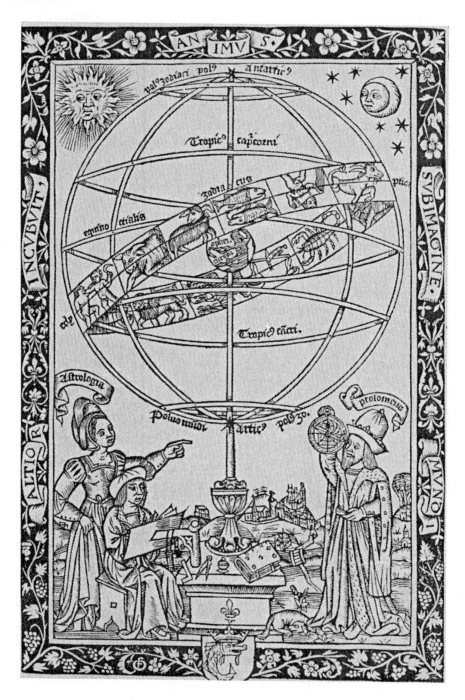

CHART 3

SIGN	GLYPH	SYMBOL	RULER	GLYPH	BODY	ELEMENT	POLARITY	KEY
Aries	♈	Ram	Mars	♂	Head	Fire	Yang	I am
Taurus	♉	Bull	Venus	♀	Neck	Earth	Yin	I have
Gemini	♊	Twin	Mercury	☿	Arms	Air	Yang	I think
Cancer	♋	Crab	Moon	☽	Breast	Water	Yin	I feel
Leo	♌	Lion	Sun	☉	Heart	Fire	Yang	I will
Virgo	♍	Virgin	Mercury	☿	Solar plexus	Earth	Yin	I analyze
Libra	♎	Scales	Venus	♀	Kidney	Air	Yang	I balance
Scorpio	♏	Scorpion	Pluto	♇	Sex Organs	Water	Yin	I desire
Ophiuchus	⛎	Caduceus	Pluto	♇	Subtle Body	Ether	Yin	I heal
Sagittarius	♐	Archer	Jupiter	♃	Thighs	Fire	Yang	I understand
Capricorn	♑	Goat	Saturn	♄	Bones	Earth	Yin	I use
Aquarius	♒	Water bearer	Uranus	♅	Ankles	Air	Yang	I know
Pisces	♓	Fishes	Neptune	♆	Feet	Water	Yin	I believe

CHART 4

INTRODUCTION
A New Sun Sign

*My evenings are taken up very largely with astrology. I
make horoscopic calculations in order to find a clue to the
core of psychological truth.*
—Carl G. Jung, in a letter to Sigmund Freud

Do you know there are now thirteen signs in the zodiac? Do you know
that you have a new sun sign? Do you know it has an immense impact on
you? Probably not, but you do know there are lots of changes going on
that you can see, feel and sense. As you look around, you know things are
changing. Some of us are apprehensive. Some of us are filled with
excitement and anticipation. Others fear change.

The purpose of this book is to explain these changes, and how they
have been set into motion by the entry of Ophiuchus into the Zodiac.

For some magical reason, the Sun, the Moon, the Stars and all the
planets in our solar system have a mysterious parallelism and
correspondence with each of our individual psyches. How and why is this
so? I am not sure. However, the ancients say that the planets are signs
from the gods to be used as tools to aid us during our journey through life.
According to the Bible, when God created the planets and stars he said,
"Let them be for signs." I say: we have a new sign in our zodiac, and it's
activated by the planet Pluto.

I first heard of this phenomenal event around Valentine's Day in 1995.
An astrologer friend called to tell me that The Royal Astronomical Society
in England had just announced the existence of a 13th astrological sign,
Ophiuchus. She went on to say that the year would have to be divided up
differently, and we would all be dislodged.

"Who am I?" I said, thinking that I must fall under this new sign.

"You are now a Pisces," she replied.

I had always been a true Aries, with all the positive and negative traits
of this sign in full-blown. As a redhead, I even looked like an Aries. I
loved the fiery energy of adventure that Aries gave me, and, true to my
sign, I hated routine. Aries is ruled by Mars (the Roman god of war), and I
needed to be up and doing things all the time with great enthusiasm, quick
wit and quick temper—mostly quick temper. I had no time or patience for

1

anybody or anything. This impatience got me into trouble more than once, but I didn't care. I loved taking risks and living dangerously. When driving my car, I imagined that I was Sterling Moss (one of the greatest Grand Prix racers).

But when I discovered that I was now a Pisces, it felt like an arrow going through my Aries heart. I couldn't think of anything more opposite or distasteful because Pisces was so patient and soulful. As a perpetual student of the art of astrology, I had to start my quest to find out how anyone could just suddenly become a Pisces.

Now that time has passed, I am the first to admit that I have started to develop the coloring of Pisces. I have gone from the "me first," cardinal fire energy of Aries to the humble, mutable, watery energy of compassionate, introspective, sensitive and dreamy characteristics of Pisces. At first, all I could think was: "My God, am I going to drown in the emotions of Pisces?" But I am a better person for the Piscean traits and colorings that I am developing. I don't know how anyone tolerated me before! Just like a child, I was clueless and self-involved. Aries, the first sign in the Zodiac, is in essence a child, while Pisces, the last sign, has the wisdom and patience of age.

This book-which I couldn't have written without the humility, patience and creativity of Pisces—will explain all the changes you may have been experiencing recently. It will attempt to give you a clearer picture and a deeper understanding of some of the new energies coming in from the shift, personally and universally, as we raise our vibrational level and move into the next (fourth) level of consciousness and awareness.

Ophiuchus is not making this happen, (we have free will) but rather is bearing witness to our changes. So far this is just the beginning of our transition into the new millennium and our transformation to the Fourth and Fifth Dimensions. We have picked an exciting time in which to live - to see all these changes taking place. Time will be speeding up even more than before, measured not in New York Minutes but in World Minutes. You will find things changing so fast that you can't help but to see the oneness in all of this. We are the people of the planet earth. Until we achieve that oneness, we will not be able to travel inter-galactic ally.

From the stars we see that our position in the Zodiac has changed to include the 13th sign. What does this change mean? That's what this book is about. The adjustments that most all of us are going through can be explained by examining the planets. The activation of Ophiuchus by Pluto has dislodged almost all of our sun signs and rearranged the Zodiac so that we must now include this 13th sign. In the same way that it is impossible not to include computers and their technologies in your life today, you will be affected by this extraordinary astrological change.

This means that we still remain who we are, but by some metaphysical mysteries of the universe, we will be given all the additional strengths and challenges of another sun sign in addition to the ones given to us at birth.

At first you may cringe at the thought, as I did. But Aries certainly could use some Piscine traits to be better equipped to evolve into the next dimension. Pisces will need Aquarius, and the Aquarian will need Capricorn, and so forth. Gemini, you are now a GemTaurian; Libra you are now a LibVirian (see Chapter 3).

Your only choice is that of participating in these changes knowingly or unknowingly.

Your evolution into the fourth dimension will go more smoothly and quickly if you know what is happening and why. Astrology has been around since the beginning of human existence. At its worst, it is a misleading and twisted parlor game filled with mystical garbage. At its best, it is an ancient tool - a vehicle for self-discovery for a better understanding of who we are and where this journey of life is taking us. The goal of this book is to help you understand and adjust to all of these new changes. Take what feels right to you in the pages ahead, and leave the rest. I like to use the "aha" factor. When you discover a new truth about something, there is almost always a confirming "aha," a shift of awareness that is both physically felt in the body and perceived in the mind.

As you read through the following chapters, some of the information may surprise you. Other information will simply confirm hunches you've had for some time. Either way, my hope is that you will embrace, in your mind, heart, and body, this powerful new time in your life. Knowing that nothing you are about to read is true, in the three dimensional sense, but it is exactly what is happening right now.

As Seen In
The New York Sunday Times Magazine
Sunday, February,19, 1995
Endpaper
The 13th Sign

When the discovery of the 13th was first announced, lots of different newspapers and news stations covered it. Some questioned, as I did, asking, "Who am I now?' Others made jokes. Still others reported it as another news item.

Ophiuchus, (Johann Bayer, Uranometria, 1603)
The 13th Sign of the Zodiac

Part One
"Meet Ophiuchus"
The 13th Sign

CHAPTER ONE
What Is This Thirteenth Sign?

There is no doubt about it that Astrology of some sort or another
will be the last achievement of Astronomy.
—Samuel Taylor Coleridge

Its name is Ophiuchus and it is a sun sign. Ophiuchus is a constellation. Ophiuchus touches all of us.

To begin with, there are 13 signs instead of twelve in the Zodiac, so that shifts all of us. A chosen few will have Ophiuchus as their new sun sign. Others may have Ophiuchus as their new rising sign or have their moon in Ophiuchus. You may have some of your personal planets (Mercury, Venus, Mars) or your social planets (Jupiter, Saturn) or your generational planets (Uranus, Neptune, Pluto) in Ophiuchus. All of us will have planets transiting Ophiuchus, just as we have planets transiting the other twelve sun signs in the twelve different houses while making different aspects to each other (square, conjunct, trine, and opposition).

Where does one start to explain the significance of Ophiuchus? Astrologers generally hate to have you bring up the name Ophiuchus because it signifies change. We often say that we want change, but when it comes right down to it, people tend to be wary of the unfamiliar.

Astronomers (unlike most astrologers) know the importance of Ophiuchus and that it is the 13th sign in the zodiac. The physical evidence is there, up in the sky. Of course, most astronomers think astrologers are crazy for not looking up at the stars every once in a while instead of always having their noses buried in the *Ephemeris* (a book listing the planets' location for any given year.) Astrology can't live in a vacuum. Astrology needs to draw from what is going on in the world, here and now. Including Ophiuchus in the Zodiac is important, and many astronomers know and understand the metaphysics and the mythology of the stars and understand the significance they play. Bridges are being built daily between physics and metaphysics. Astronomers know that the stars and the moon do reflect what is happening on earth. It is essential that we rebuild the bridge between astrologers and astronomers, and Ophiuchus would be a great place to start. For thousands of years, astrology, astronomy and medicine were all one science called "The Art," they were

9

separated only in the last few centuries by the involvement of churches and governments.

Just try to imagine the scope of the wisdom that could be achieved if astrology, astronomy and medicine were all working together again as "The Art," especially with today's technologies.

Ophiuchus Is Being Brought To You By Pluto

To help you understand where Ophiuchus is and why it is now activated, we have to look at Pluto. Planets don't always follow the exact path around the sun, just as people don't always do everything the exact same way. In 1930, as a result of the observation of irregularities in the motions of Uranus and Neptune, Pluto was discovered in the constellation of Cancer. Astrologers and astronomers think that it takes about 246 years for Pluto to travel around the sun and through the different Zodiac Signs.

Pluto has an eccentric and erratic orbit; it can stay in an astrological sign anywhere between thirteen and thirty-two years. Therefore, no living person has ever seen Pluto in Sagittarius. In 1995, astrologers were expecting Pluto to go into Sagittarius as predicted by *Ephemeris*, but it didn't happen. Pluto went into a sign called Ophiuchus, which is between Scorpio and Sagittarius (see chart on pages 19,20.)

On January 20, 1995, CNN announced that "there being 13, instead of 12, Zodiac signs generated quite a stir in the astrological world today." Pluto, the planet of transformation (see Pluto traits page 127) brought in Ophiuchus and the need to transcend some of the differences between astrology and astronomy. "The Universe," wrote Albert Einstein, "is stranger than we know."

Who is Ophiuchus, The Serpent Holder?

Knowing the mythology of Ophiuchus will help you understand why and how he fits into this New Age of Transformation. When we read mythology, the stories vary slightly from source to source. Therefore, I have taken most of my information from the most accessible and best-known source, the Compton's Encyclopedia.

Ophiuchus is derived from the Greek words for "Serpent Holder." The ancient Greeks considered Ophiuchus to be the image of Aesculapius (in Latin, Asclepius), the God of Medicine. Aesculapius was the son of the gods Apollo and Coronis, who was raised by the wise centaur, Chiron. Chiron taught the boy about botany, medicine and the practice of healing. Aesculapius became very knowledgeable about various herbs and plants and was a true student of nature. One day, while at a friend's house, Aesculapius killed a snake. He then watched in astonishment when a companion snake slithered into the room with a particular herb in its mouth and restored the slain snake to life. Recognizing the plant, Aesculapius soon learned to use its mystical powers to heal the sick and resurrect the dead.

It is from this legend and from the ability of a snake to cast off its skin and assume a kind of rebirth that the serpent became the symbol of healing. The staff of Aesculapius, with the snake curled around it, is known today as the symbol of Western medicine, the caduceus.

Aesculapius, the first doctor, sailed off on the famous voyage of the Argonauts in search of the Golden Fleece. Aesculapius quickly became a gifted healer and eventually learned to bring the dead back to life. Upon the death of Orion, Ophiuchus was about to restore life to Orion when Hades (Pluto), the god of the underground, stopped him by appealing to his brother Zeus (Jupiter). He claimed that his realm of the underworld would decline if Aesculapius was allowed to go around raising the dead.

Zeus (Jupiter, brother of Pluto) agreed that death should be the ultimate end of mortal man, not to be trifled with, not even by the most skilled of physicians. When Zeus saw Ophiuchus taking money for curing people, Zeus, the King of the gods, struck Aesculapius with a thunderbolt that ended his life on earth. Apollo, Aesculapuis' father, protested the execution of his son, whereupon Zeus placed Aesculapius among the stars as a tribute to the accomplishments and skills of this great physician. There Aesculapuis is known as "Ophiuchus" the Serpent Bearer.

Isn't it appropriate, then, that Pluto—the planet of transformation—transforms the Zodiac by bringing in Ophiuchus and placing Ophiuchus in the Eighth House, which he (Pluto) rules? The Eighth House deals with death, rebirth, and other people's money.

11

Where in the Heavens is Ophiuchus?

In astronomy, Ophiuchus is a large but relatively faint constellation. It stretches across the celestial equator. Consequently, it can be observed from almost any part of the world. In the United States from spring to fall, at a 10 p.m. observation of the sky in mid-latitude, Ophiuchus first appears in the east in April, reaches its greatest height in the sky in July, and drops below the western horizon in October. Ophiuchus is a very old constellation. The star figure was recognized by the Sumerians as early as the 3rd millennium BC. But now with the activation by Pluto, Ophiuchus ought to be included as a sun sign. The sun does transit Ophiuchus.

Ophiuchus is between the constellations of Sagittarius and Scorpio in the Zodiac. In the constellation Ophiuchus, the stars form the outline of a man holding a snake that stretches out eastward. Its name is Serpens Cauda. Westward, it is called Serpens Caput. (See chart on page 19). The brightest star, Alphia (in the head of Ophiuchus), bears the ancient Arabic name of Ras al Hagus, which means "the head of him who holds." The Greek name Ophiuchus is, itself, from the Hebrew and Arabic name Afeichus, which means, "the serpent held." Barnard's Star is also found in the constellation of Ophiuchus. The Barnard Star was always thought to have its own planets (for further information, see page 161).

Why Must We Change?

Socrates (470-399 B.C.) wrote, "Nothing ever is, but all things are becoming ... All things are the offspring of flux and motion." In the same vein, Marcus Aurelius (121-180 A.D.) wrote, "Observe how all things are continually being born of change. Whatever is, is in the same sense the seed to what is to emerge from it."

The only thing guaranteed on this planet is change. There is no death. We may lose our bodies, but we still remain who we are. Our bodies are only our visual energy vibration on this third and fourth dimension planet, but they are not us. In other words, our bodies are among the tools we use on this learning planet called Earth. Nothing ends; it only changes, for there is just a continuum of change. We are changing all the time. We can almost feel our bodies changing.

Our minds are expanding as never before. We can get information on anything in seconds from a computer. But in time, we will not even need the computer. We will be able to tap into the Universal Collective Unconscious, perhaps not right now but eventually, in the Fourth and Fifth dimensions. We only use about three percent of our brain right now. (See Chapter 2.) We are taking a giant step, a leap in time right now. The old ways are going by the wayside because they don't work anymore, not in technology nor in medicine. Even the horoscope charts I do for other people have shifted. The charts have evolved so much that I must use the 13th sign of Ophiuchus or the chart is off; some information is missing.

It's like doing a chart and leaving out Pluto - that is the only way I can explain it. You can do a reading without Pluto, but look at what is missing! Pluto, the planet of transformation, is in everyone's chart. Astrologers look for the location of Pluto to see where the biggest changes are going to take place in people's lives (currently, Pluto is in Ophiuchus. It has been since 1995 and will probably stay there for another 10 or 15 years). Another example is Chiron, which only a few astrologers use, because it is a newcomer that was discovered in 1977. But once you start using Chiron, it's hard to not to want to know the Chiron input.

On the other hand, when astrologers factor in the 13th sign, Ophiuchus, in their calculations and predictions for a client's chart, the readings are more consonant with what's actually happening in the client's life. The readings are far more accurate, and so is the timing of events.

Astrology works with the energies that are available at the time. The energy of Ophiuchus is here now, and it is only going to get stronger. In the future, there will be other signs coming in as we transform and evolve.

As we move into this new millennium at lighting speed, we are changing and living many lives in our lifetime. For example, our grandparents didn't have the technology for television, and now the whole world is open to us via the Internet, cell phones, cable television and jet airplanes. The world has become a global village in which we have multiple identities - many of us are Italian-Irish or Jewish-Buddhist. A person can be an astrologer, a writer, a teacher, a stock investor, a skier, an artist, a cook, a parent, and so on.

We are becoming multi-cultural even as we multi-task. Think of a Saturday morning with a room full of middle-aged women from Long Island, sitting on the floor in a yoga position, chanting in Sanskrit trying to raise their kundalini (energy). Think of a Saturday afternoon on 110th

13

Street in Harlem with a busload of Japanese tourists in a Baptist Church singing gospel songs. Think of the once-called hillbillies in the Appalachian Mountains hooked into a satellite dish accessing 310 different channels. Think of truck drivers trading stock on laptop computers at a truck stop on the road. We are experiencing so much more than was ever available before.

The world is evolving, and so are we. Astrology works with energies. There is more energy coming in from the cosmos than ever before—because the earth is traveling back to the center of the Zodiac. (See Chapter 2, page 26). To be better equipped for the complexities of 21st Century life, we need to carry two different sun sign energies. I must display the Piscine traits of being humble, compassionate, sympathetic, kind and intuitive, along with my Arian traits of being pioneering, competitive, impulsive and courageous.

I am living many lives at once. I am the mother, the housekeeper, the healer and the artist. I am also the writer, the astrologer, the traveler, the lover, the friend, the lecturer, the teacher, the gardener and the little girl inside the mature woman who made it through the 1960's and will make it through this transition into the fourth dimension.

Just two hundred years ago few people traveled beyond their own villages. Few people finished school, and fewer people read books—things we take for granted today. Like everything else, astrological charts have to change and grow.

The 13th Sign: Ophiuchus

Pluto is showing our transformation with the activation of the 13th sign. We are now expanding beyond the twelve-sign astrological chart. We see this fact portrayed in legends and mythology, the 13th being that realized individual. We see this with the 12 tribes of Israel, the 12 apostles of Jesus, the 12 labors of Hercules, and the 12 knights of King Arthur's Round Table. The 13th being is that individual who has gone through the 12 different phases, 12 different functions, and 12 different Zodiac signs and integrated them into his or her being. It is that individual who has risen above his or her ego centered personality and has come to the point of the actualized self.

That which develops does not stop growing; it becomes part of a continuum. Ophiuchus is the 13th sign that will show our growth into the god self, the realized self, and help us evolve. Ophiuchus is adding another dimension to the astrological chart as we are transforming into the fourth dimension. Now is the time for us to take that giant leap into the New Age and rise above our ego centered self. It is the time to release our fears of limitations.

Both the Old and New Testaments open with powerful statements about the validity of astrology. According to the Bible (Genesis 1:14), when God created the planets and stars he said, "Let them be for signs," as was mentioned earlier. In the New Testament, when Jesus was born, "wise men from the East" saw a star signaling the birth of a great soul and set out for Jerusalem to find Him (Matthew 2:1-2).

Ophiuchus is like that. It is being activated as the light out of our darkness by Pluto. It is a sign for our evolution. Is Pluto bringing in Ophiuchus as a sign of the beginning of a rebirth? Ophiuchus comes with the answers of life and death. Ophiuchus comes holding the Serpent. Is he symbolizing Adam from the Garden of Eden with the Serpent inviting us to take from the Tree of Knowledge? Is the Apple the computer? Will it teach and connect us all as one on the physical plane as well as the astral plane? Is it here to come to tell us—like Bell's commercial-that we are all connected? Or is it here to show us that life never ends?

The serpent is found in Eastern religions too. One must raise the kundalini, or serpent inside us, in order to awaken to our spiritual potential. Kundalini the divine, conscious energy inside everyone that is awakens through meditation. The energy rises inside the body making a coiled snake figure. C.G. Jung also suggested that the Serpent represents the Higher Self, the Jungian Self, and the Christ Consciousness.

We are beginning to realize who we are on a soul level of consciousness while maintaining the awareness of our physical bodies. As Johannes Kepler (1571-1630) wrote in *De Stella Nova*, "Nothing exists nor happens in the visible sky that is not sensed in some hidden moment by the faculties of Earth and nature."

But Why Ophiuchus?

Ophiuchus, the serpent holder, is the healer, the doctor, and the rejuvenator. If we are to evolve, so must our physical bodies as well as our awareness, not only of our bodies' needs, but also their purpose. Our bodies are more than a place to house us, or a temple to keep our mind and soul. Our bodies are also precious gifts and incredible tools for experiencing and learning.

Ever since Pluto moved out of Scorpio and went into Ophiuchus in 1995, many discoveries and new inroads in medicine have been made. If you had money in the stock market and invested in pharmaceutical and biotech companies, your investments would have shown tremendous activity. All kinds of new companies, new medicines, and new cures are available. Some alternative forms of medicine are being covered by HMOs. Physicians and hospitals are beginning to open to the possibilities of all kinds of alternative ways of being healed. New York Presbyterian Medical Center is one of the leaders in this area by allowing Reiki healers in the operating room. Health care is changing faster than we can keep up with it. A friend of mine who is a hand-on-healer shares office space with a group of medical doctors in Darien, Connecticut, and she is there at their request. Our physical bodies need all the help they can get because they are housing the ever-expanding mind and soul.

Pluto activated Ophiuchus to show the new energies available to strengthen the body and change our belief system about our bodies' we can move into the Aquarian Age, to the fourth dimension. Ophiuchus has been brought into the Zodiac to show that the teacher of healing and wholeness is ourselves and to make us aware of just what finely tuned instruments our bodies are - instruments that must work in conjunction with our minds and spirits.

Ophiuchus: The Teacher of Healing and Wholeness

Ophiuchus is not just confined to the eighth house of death and rebirth. Ophiuchus is affecting every one of us. Ophiuchus has shifted the whole Zodiac, giving us the quality of another sun sign in conjunction with our original sun sign (or by doubling our original characteristics). Bringing into focus our weakest qualities, it shows us the energies needed to transform these weaknesses into strengths. Thus, it teaches us our own healing through wholeness.

For about 75 percent of us, Ophiuchus is also bringing the Yin and Yang together. Every sign in the Zodiac is masculine or feminine. Therefore, if you were in the masculine sign such as Aries, you will now be combining the feminine sign, Pisces. Taurus, being feminine, will be bringing the masculine sign of Aries.

This alchemy mix of the Yin and Yang balance is needed for most of us to complete our wholeness. A small percentage of the Zodiac will be needing the double masculine or feminine for a time to continue the journey on which they have set forth. The double feminine signs will truly use their feminine intuition and insight to help materialize what is needed to support the planet through this transition. The double masculine signs have incredible business acumen and know how to get things done. Trust these attributes. They will help you accomplish things and build a new future.

Basic Qualities of Ophiuchus:

- ☐ Ophiuchus: The Serpent Holder
- ☐ Time: November 30 to December 17 (18 days)
- ☐ Element: ether
- ☐ Quality: fixed
- ☐ Ruler: Pluto
- ☐ Anatomy: the third eye and subtle body
- ☐ Key Phase: I Heal
- ☐ Keywords: revitalization, regeneration, rejuvenation, rebirth
- ☐ Symbol: the man holding a snake
- ☐ Glyph: the staff of Aesculapius, with a serpent coiling around its staff.
- ☐ House: eight house/ shared
- ☐ Color: clear/white (light from the darkness)
- ☐ Stone: quartz crystal, the healing stone
- ☐ Flower: lily (symbol of rebirth)
- ☐ Function: feeling

17

Positive Characteristics: Healing, helpful, considerate, scientific, scholarly, clean green thumb, adaptable, respectful, strong immune system, intuitive, spiritual, progressive thinker, nonjudgmental, and loving

Negative Characteristics: Overbearing, high-and-mighty, sickly, angry, closed-minded, noncommittal, self indulgent, impatient, sloppy, tactless, greedy.

There are two sides to everything on this planet. For every day, there is a night. Let us keep the force positive. You can go through this transformation in pain or in joy. The choice is yours.

Aim point RA: 16h 51m Dec: -12°21'25"
Wed 2001 Oct 31 0:15 UTC
http://www.fourmilab,ch/cgi-bin/uncgi/Yourtel

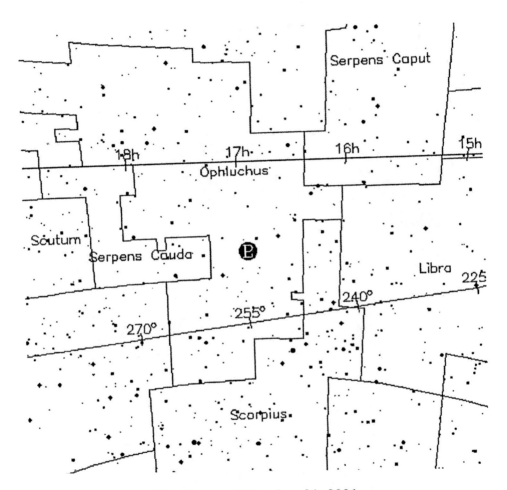

The sky as of October 31, 2001
Note: The location of Pluto - It is in Ophiuchus
(See drawing of Ophiuchus on next page)

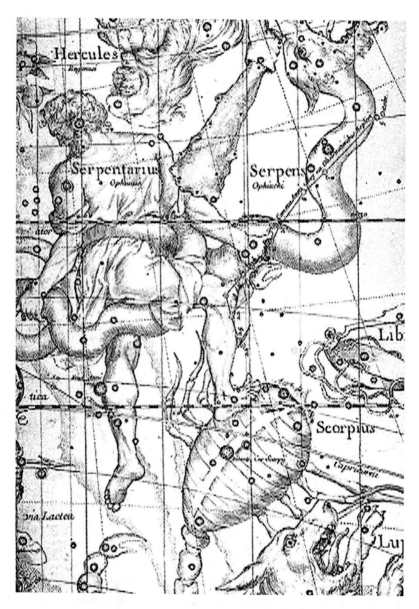

Ophiuchus,/Serpentarius - (Pardies, Paris 1674)
Note: Location Pluto in Ophiuchus (check previous page)

CHAPTER TWO
Astrology and Ophiuchus

*Love cures people, the ones who receive love and the ones
who give it too.*
Karl Augustus Menninger

Astrology is constantly changing and evolving. With the advent of powerful telescopes, satellites, and technology, there will be many changes in astrology as well as in astronomy. Throughout the history of astrology, there have been sporadic periods of intense activity and growth.

With the transcendental planet Uranus ushering in the Aquarian Age, the unexpected is expected (Uranus in Aquarius 1995-2002), especially in science, astrology, computers and bringing forward our awareness into the laws of the universe.

Astrology is a tool given to us by the ancients to help fulfill our greatest wants and needs. It encourages the passion to find out who we are, where are we going, how to get there and when. Throughout history, cultures and religions have looked to the stars for information, trying to find the meaning and purpose of life. References to the stars are repeated over and over again in both the Old and New Testaments of the Bible.

Astrology is a gift filled with symbols, images and mythology. The symbols are the planets, which represent the energy available to us: Mercury, Venus, Mars, Jupiter, Saturn, Uranus, Neptune and Pluto (also the Sun and the Moon). The images are the astrological signs and the pattern in which the energy forms: Aries, Taurus, Gemini, Cancer, Leo, Virgo, Libra, Scorpio, Ophiuchus, Sagittarius, Capricorn, Aquarius and Pisces. The mythology is the stories being played out in the twelve different houses of the astrological chart where the energy (planets) and pattern (astrological signs) take place.

The true treasure in astrology is *not* the ability to predict but, rather, the power to reveal the abilities that dwell in each of us. The old textbook way of doing astrology is gone. Now the astrologer works with energies to see the bigger picture. The astrologer uses intuition and physic knowledge. (The Art of Astrology is about your alchemistic ability to blend layer upon layer of information until you have integrated all the symbols, all the energies, aspects and cycles with your own inner knowingness.)

21

Your inner knowingness or psychic ability is something we all have and the more we use it, the more it grows. Soon you will find that all the calculations will just flow into an exact and precise understanding of how the big picture of your life is being played out.

The Aspects—angled degrees between planets and/or houses in the astrological chart—show us the different connections and energies between the planets that will aid us in our choices. The aspects are changing all the time, reflecting the available energy. One of the easiest and best ways to understand astrology is to understand the myths and the archetypal images of the myths associated with the stars. It seems that the internal stories that we are playing out in our lives are "like unto" the stories in the myths. By some inexplainable means, the planets are synchronistic reflections of what is going on in our psyches. The perfect example of myth and metaphor played out in modern life was the Y2K crisis. The beginning of the new millennium, the starting of the Aquarian Age, is a time for a major "upgrade" of our human consciousness. If we don't upgrade, our lives will fall apart. It is time to open our Third Eye (see page 98) and expand our minds. This upgrade, I believe, was being shown in the sky by Pluto in Ophiuchus and on earth as the Y2K scare.

As we evolve, so do astronomy and astrology. The Planet of Uranus was not discovered by astronomers until 1781. Neptune was discovered in 1846. Pluto was discovered in 1930. One of the newest discoveries is Chiron, identified by scientists in 1977. If we go back to the myth of Ophiuchus, Chiron and Pluto played important roles. Isn't it fitting for the stage to be set by Pluto and Chiron for the entrance of Ophiuchus? Ophiuchus is a major part of the new awareness that realizes the human potential and then expands it. On the eve of the new millennium, Pluto and Chiron aligned in the sky in Ophiuchus, not Sagittarius, giving this conjunction enormous impact for profound transformation. There is a great deal of symbolism in this in that we, as the people of the earth, collectively conscious or unconscious, are ready for this change in our reality.

I believe it is Ophiuchus that is reflecting the opening of our conscience and expanding our perception of life.

Why Is Ophiuchus Appearing Now?

Why now? Why not 2,000 years ago? Why not 5,000 years from now? To give a partial explanation, the procession of the equinoxes and the earth's wobble play an important part in this.

(Please refer to the diagram on page 26, to make this easier to follow.)

The earth has a 23½-degree tilt. This tilt gives us our seasons. At the celestial equator, the plane of the Earth's equator cuts through the celestial sphere (or the imaginary sphere on which we have the zodiac-see chart). The axis of the Earth is wobbling in a way that shifts the equinoctial points to about one degree every seventy years. Therefore, every 2,000 years the equinoctial points move into a different zodiac constellation. This 2,000 year time span is called a Platonic Month. At the millennium, we went from the Piscine Age to the Aquarian Age. About every 25,900 years, we have one full wobble or one full circle around the zodiac. This almost 26,000 year time span is called a Platonic Year.

Platonic Year. From 8000-6000 B.C., the platonic year was called the Age of Cancer; 6000- 4000 B.C. was the Age of Gemini; 4000-2000 B.C. was the Age of Taurus; and 2000 B.C. the year zero was the Age. Zero to 2000 A.D. was the Age of Pisces—symbol the fishes. And the symbol the fishes is also related to Christianity.

Now it is the Age of Aquarius (2000-4000 A.D), symbol for which is The Water Bearer. Water represents the unconscious; the bearer pouring water represents the opening of the unconscious.

The tip of the North Pole traces an ellipse. One point of the ellipse is close to the center of our galaxy; the other is farther away (see chart). Originally this wobble was not taken into account due to lack of knowledge. Now, however, the astronomers know about the wobble because of the technology they use to watch and study the sky.

Unfortunately, many of my fellow astrologers have not kept their art up to date. Astrologers must get their noses out of the *Ephemeris* and look up to the sky to see where the planets are. Astrology and astronomy were once combined, and should be again.

What the Ancients Say

Notably, the Hindus and Tibetans say that as we travel away from the center of the galaxy we fall asleep, and as we arc back again, we wake up (see page 26) Our most asleep point was 2,000 years ago. That is why many believe that Jesus was sent to wake us to see the light of Christ, the Christ-conscious, or, as Carl Gustav Jung would say, the "realized self."

Follow this carefully. The earth travels around the sun. We fall asleep at night and we wake up in the morning. Instead of every 24 hours, it takes about 26,000 years for the earth to make the zodiac circle. Seen in this light, we have been "asleep" for about 4,000 years. (See on page 26)

As has been said, we use about only three percent of our brains; some scientific theorists claim that we use 10 percent. Either way, it is as if we are walking around in a dream state. We think we are fully awake, but we are over 90 percent asleep.

Working with a scale of seven levels of consciousness, we are on the third level. When we dream, we are on the second level of consciousness; and when we are completely out and unable to awaken, that is the first level. When we are dreaming on the second level of consciousness, we believe what we are experiencing is true until we awaken. The same goes for the third level of consciousness. As we move more into the new millennium, age of Aquarius, we will be moving into the fourth and fifth level of consciousness and the fourth dimension. The earth is fourth dimensional now, but most of us are still living in the third dimension.

In some regard, we already know this. In fact, we know everything. But we can't remember, because, as has already been stated, we only use a very small percentage of our brains. This is why many of the things that I am saying will resonate with you - will "ring a bell." This is because you are *remembering*, rather than learning something new. This is also why I like working with the *aha!* factor; it is a form of recollection. Plato stated that; "All learning is recollection."

As we move into the fourth dimension, we remove another veil to the unconsciousness. There are seven veils or seven layers of consciousness. It is the dance of life. (Removing a veil is becoming more aware, being able to see from a different or higher perspective.) Many of the Eastern religions talk about levels of consciousness. The Earth has now moved into the fourth dimension, and we are still shifting back and forth from the third to the fourth level of consciousness. When we see synchronicity in things, we are working in the fourth dimension. We hope that we will all be living in the fourth level of consciousness on this fourth dimension planet Earth within the next 10 to15 years.

If we look far back in history, we can find evidence of many unexplained superior civilizations. At Tiahuanaco, Peru, the center of Incan culture, the remains of calendar tablets giving the exact positions of the Moon every hour was discovered recently. Noted archeologist Jim Allen claims: that the tablets could date back as far as, 12,000 BC, the time of Atlantis. The tablets and other findings also showed astronomical symbols giving planetary positions of the procession of the equinoxes of some 26,000 years.

Another astonishing fact is that the ancient Mayans of Mexico, whose advanced culture displayed an understanding of the heavens, showed the precise orbit of Venus as well as Uranus and Neptune. This is astonishing, because Uranus was not discovered by the Western world until 1781—with a telescope—Let's look back to the Egyptian pyramids. I believe that early Egyptians knew we were "falling asleep"-that is, using less of our brain. The Egyptians started writing in hieroglyphs, knowing that we, the people of the earth, were losing our abilities to access the full mind and to tap into the collective consciousness. We were moving backward, from the fifth to the fourth to the third dimensions. Finally, we needed to spell everything out as we have in this third dimension.

Today, as we move forward into the fourth and fifth dimensions, we are using hieroglyphs again because more is understood with one simple symbol than with 100 words. Just look at the hieroglyphs all over the computer. We don't need all the words and language barriers; we are beginning to speak in universal symbols and with fuller understanding.

We are beginning to wake up. As we start to awaken, we notice the quickening of communication. We need fewer words to convey a thought, yet we have more words to use. Look at all the new words or words changing their meaning, which have come into our vocabulary in the past few years because of the computer and the Internet (i.e., e-mail, s-mail, online, Ethernet, broadband, CD, mouse). As we use more of our brain, we will use fewer words, because much more information will be conveyed telepathically. Right now, we are experiencing an explosion of words. When the dust settles, we will have a universal language. It will be made up of hieroglyphs, not much different from the Egyptians' drawing on the walls, but today's "hieroglyphs" brought to us by computers. Today we can talk on a cell phone to any place in the world. Not too many years ago, that would have been a miracle. In the fourth and fifth dimensions, we won't need a cell phone to talk to people. We will just communicate, and it won't be a miracle!

The awakening that we are experiencing is symbolized by Ophiuchus in the heavens. Ophiuchus was activated by Pluto, the planet of transformation. The Egyptians, being extremely influenced by astrology, built the Pyramids perfectly aligned with the stars. The greatest of all the Pyramids in Giza is aligned with Ophiuchus. Ophiuchus is an important player and is now in the Zodiac.

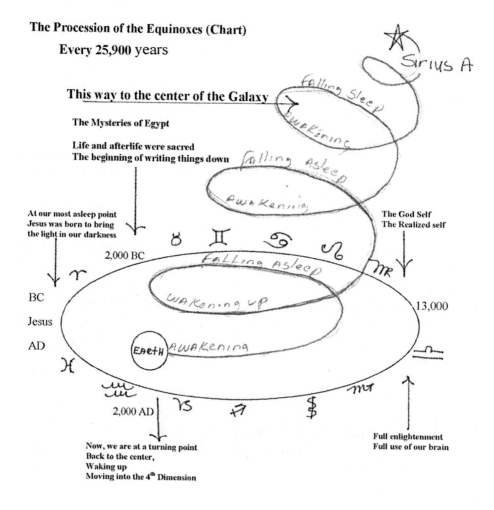

The Procession of the Equinoxes (Chart)

Every 25,900 years

This way to the center of the Galaxy

The Mysteries of Egypt

Life and afterlife were sacred
The beginning of writing things down

At our most asleep point
Jesus was born to bring
the light in our darkness

2,000 BC

BC

Jesus

AD

The God Self
The Realized self

13,000

Full enlightenment
Full use of our brain

2,000 AD

Now, we are at a turning point
Back to the center,
Waking up
Moving into the 4th Dimension

26

The Ancient Greeks: Hippocrates and Ophiuchus

Hippocrates is the Greek "Father of Medicine"; Ophiuchus is the Greek "god of Medicine." Hippocrates is the 15th grandson of Ophiuchus (Asclepius). Hippocrates lived in Greece in the "Golden Century" (about 460 - 377 BC). He was born on the island of Kos. He was the son of a doctor named Heraklides, whose family produced many well-known physicians, dating back to Aesculapius, Latin, or Asclepius, Greek (Ophiuchus.)   Hippocrates was a contemporary of the philosopher Socrates and was written about by Plato and Aristotle. There are a number of writings ascribed to Hippocrates that are known in our present time. The works differ greatly, in their length, subject matter and intent. Some of his teachings were for physicians, some for assistants and students, some for lay-people, and a few were for philosophers. Remember that in Hippocrates' time a physician was also an astrologer and astronomer who took care of the whole body as well as the subtle body. (The subtle body is our invisible/overbody that carries all our karma/experiences and memories-see Chapter 4.) "A physician without knowledge of Astrology," Hippocrates said, "has no right to call himself a physician." The most ancient code of medical ethics is found in the Hippocratic Oath, which is still taken by medical students, whatever their specialty, upon graduation.

He further warned, "Touch not with metal that part of the body ruled by the sign the Moon is transiting." Most contemporary medical professionals ignore this astrological wisdom of their founding father and have no clue as to how to interpret his words. This dictum means: One does not perform a surgical procedure with a knife upon a part of the patient's body which is ruled by the astrological sign that the moon is transiting at that time. The Moon travels through all the signs of the zodiac each month, remaining in one sign approximately two and a half days each month. (See page 29.)

According to Hippocrates, disobeying this law will inevitably result in one of these outcomes:

1. 1.Complication, including infection;
2. 2.Unusually slow and painful healing and recuperation: or
3. 3.Death.

Outcomes No. 1 and No. 2 are more likely. But nevertheless, listening to the warning of Hippocrates is clearly the wise thing to do.

Doctors and hospitals estimate that five to ten percent of all deaths in hospitals are unexplained. Perhaps if doctors understood Hippocrates' wisdom before taking the oath, that five percent of patients could have been saved. If only the doctors had an astrology class, they might understand the influence of the moon. With Ophiuchus changing things, this could happen. The doctors could apply what most of us know; that the moon affects us. We all know the effect the moon has upon the earth's tides. Our bodies are made up of eighty five percent water, and our bodies have their own internal tides. Hence, Hippocrates' surgical, lunar dictum.

Ophiuchus will change medicine. Now that Ophiuchus is activated by Pluto, the wisdom from Hippocrates must be considered. He wrote in his diaries that, "He who practices medicine without the benefit of the movement of the stars and planets is a fool."

Surgery interrupts tidal flow in the body by the unnatural process of cutting open the body and allowing air to enter. Consequently, that part of the body, which is ruled by whatever astrological sign the moon, is traveling through at the time is especially sensitive and vulnerable (see chart).

The moon affects us in many other ways. If you want your hair to be thick and full, cut it on the full moon. To get it to grow faster cut it on the new moon or when the moon is waxing (getting larger.) If you don't want it to grow—cut it when the moon is waning (getting smaller.) It really works, (Check it out in the Farmer's Almanac.) Still skeptical? Ask a police officer in any city, and he or she will likely tell you that there is much more criminal activity when the moon is full.

Salespeople in department stores can tell you when the moon is full by the number of half-crazed customers they encounter. Even emergency room nurses and doctors will tell you that on the full moon, they are twice as busy with more babies being born, more deaths and more accidents. Many farmers plant by the movement of the moon for better, fuller, healthier crops. Astronomers and astrologers both agree that the movement of the planets and the moon have a tremendous impact on us. On this point, however, they disagree: Astronomers see that planet Pluto has moved into the zodiac sign of Ophiuchus. However, most Astrologers can't accept the visual fact that Ophiuchus is now part of the Zodiac changing things all around them. Are they blinded like modern physicians? Much internal work needs to be done by all of us. I hope that Ophiuchus, the Greek god of medicine, will bring back The Art—the craft, of the physician, the astrologer, the astronomer and the philosopher working together.

The Zodiac and Our Body

Since the beginning of the Zodiac and Astrology, each sign has a special relationship to a specific area of the body, starting with Aries at the head to Pisces at the feet.

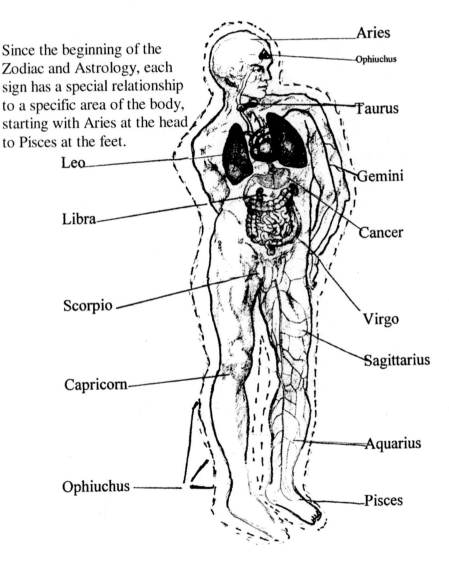

Aries

Ophiuchus

Taurus

Gemini

Leo

Cancer

Libra

Virgo

Scorpio

Sagittarius

Capricorn

Aquarius

Ophiuchus

Pisces

The god of medicine and healing.

Part Two
Your "New Sun Sign"

CHAPTER THREE
Who You Are Becoming: Traditional and New Astrological Birth Sign Dates

The unexamined life is not worth living.
-Socrates

Take a minute right now and try this exercise:

1. Think about yourself.
2. Think about your strengths.
3. Think about your weaknesses.
4. Think about how you've changed over the last several years.
5. Now check the list of new sun signs on page 37. See how the added sun (or doubling sign) matches your changes mostly for the better.
6. Think of someone you know well.
7. Think of how he or she has changed over last few years.
8. Check the list-see how the characteristics of the new sign matches his or her change.
9. Notice that what you need most to help you with your challenge/weakness is found in the new sun sign as positive your characteristics.
10. Ask someone if he or she feels or sees the changes in your characteristic traits.
11. Find out what his or her new sign is, than ask if the new traits match these changes.
12. Remember: We are still our original sun sign, but with added color and energies.

Most of the stress that we have been putting ourselves through in the last few years has occurred because we are changing; things that worked in the past no longer work. Even if we claim to want change, it is still uncomfortable and stressful. The world is awakening—so must we. If we don't, we will suffer until we do, because the energies on this planet are taking us into the Fourth Dimension. A level of existence where we become clairvoyant and see things clearly, a place where we can no longer lie to others or ourselves. It is a level, a vibration, and a state of being where we can understand and co-create everything in our world, be it good or bad.

The awakening that we are seeing and feeling, as well as the quickening of time and the development of our psyches and sense of self, must be reflected in our astrological chart as it is reflected in the heavens and within ourselves. These shifts will be for the better, be it in our love life or relationships with family, friends or business. You will now be carrying more tools in your cosmic backpack. You will be able to work with the gifts and talents of two astrological sun signs.

I can't emphasize enough that in the beginning it will be stressful and uncomfortable until you accept the fact that we are all evolving. I don't want to minimize your pain and struggle or your great highs and lows, but you have to adjust to your changes and the changes of everyone and everything around you. Yes, some relationships will break up, in love or in business. Many of us have already experienced or are experiencing this transformation. For example: That job you were planning to stay at until you retire is being eliminated, or that marriage that was made in heaven is now in hell. Or that house you've been living in (and hoped to see the mortgage paid off) will soon be sold. Or that major you planned to study in college just changed.

In hindsight, you will see just why you were going through all these emotions and transitions and realize that they were for the better. If you honestly look at them, you may see that you really were not happy. You may have found it comfortable, because you were used to it, but we can't live in the survival mode anymore. Just remember that the Earth is the learning planet. We come here to learn, and experience. You picked this time and incarnation to experience this exciting period of cosmic awakening.

Whether you see it in your everyday activity, or it's just a vague feeling inside, you know that if you don't grow, you are on the fast track to some major upheaval. You may say, "I am just me; what can I do?" But you are already doing *something*—reading this book and understanding that we are all creators of the collective conscious and unconscious, and that is what shifts this world. We are not going to be able to travel in other solar systems until all the people of the Earth understand that whatever we do and think effects every one of us; that we are the people of the earth and are not separated by color, race or religion. We must stop all this competition for the need to be bigger and better than everyone else. To know that even our thoughts put out tremendous energy and vibration can bring about transformation. (Intergalactic travel is not far off. There is other intelligent life in this and other universes. "If there isn't, it would be a terrible waste of space," said Carl Sagan of NASA.)

The planet Earth is already in the fourth dimension, we are still in the third dimension, we are shifting, as shown by the activation of Ophiuchus in the sky. This is what all this uneasiness you may be experiencing is about. Sometimes, you have to step back and observe yourself and let life live you, instead or you living life. We are all safe. Don't be afraid of change, accept it. Inside, you know it's time; otherwise Mother Earth will be without you. All she is asking you to do is be happy, find your joy. "Follow your bliss," as Joseph Campbell put it.

When Earth shifts again, into the Fifth Dimension, (some will experience it in this lifetime; I certainly hope to) if you haven't changed by then, you will not be able to handle the intense energy vibration on this planet. Already we are seeing intense anger and road rage, which is the result of unhappiness due to the energy shift on this planet Earth. But the stars are showing us that we have been given tools to help us make this adjustment. See your new sun signs as gifts and dance, reflect and enjoy.

This is your rite of passage to a happier and more joyous being. We no longer live in a linear, sequential reality. The door is open to the magic, the miracles and the synchronicity of these times, of the possibility of the impossible. As the great Sufi poet, Jelaluddin Rumi, wrote in the 13[th]century:

> This mirror inside me shows...
> I can't say what, but I can't not know!

35

Traditional Astrological Birth Sign Dates

ZODIAC SIGN	OLD DATES	# of Days
Aries	March 20 - April 18	30
Taurus	April 19 - May 20	31
Gemini	May 20 - June 19	31
Cancer	June 20 - June 21	32
Leo	July 22 - August 21	31
Virgo	August 22 - September 21	30
Libra	September 22 - October 21	30
Scorpio	October 22 - November 20	30
Sagittarius	November 21 - December 20	30
Capricorn	December 21 - January 19	30
Aquarius	January 20 - February 18	30
Pisces	February 19 - March 19	29

Your New Sign

Check out the changes—not only in the dates, but also in the length of time the sun actually remains in each sign. Scorpio has become a very exclusive sign with only seven days. Virgo with its 45 days is giving us a clear sign about which energies are increasing. Notice also the placement of Ophiuchus, between Scorpio and Sagittarius.

NEW SUN SIGN	NEW DATES	#Of DAYS
The New Pisces	March 12-April 18	38
The New Aries	April 19-May13	25
The New Taurus	May 14-June 19	37
The New Gemini	June 20-July 20	31
The New Cancer	July 21-August 9	20
The New Leo	August 10-September 15	37
The New Virgo	September 16-October 30	45
The New Libra	October 31-November 22	23
The New Scorpio	November 23-November 29	7
Ophluchus	November 30-December 17	18
The New Sagittarius	December 18-January 18	32
The New Capricorn	January 19-February 15	28
The New Aquarius	February 16-March 11	24

Note: You will remain your original sun sign, but now you will also have additional energies and coloring of either a new sign or double your original sign.

You Are Transforming: From Aries to AriPiscian

March 20 to April 18—The Renaissance of Aries

My Dear "AriPiscian":

There are now 38 days of Pisces that start on about March 12 and run through April 18.

This change is quite dramatic. You'll be combining the fire of Aries with the water of Pisces. With that fire and water you will make steam, and with that steam you will have powerful cosmic energies from the ethers. With these energies, you will be combining your Aries' courageous pioneering spirit, vision and insight with Pisces' great creativity, compassion and emotions. All of your actions come from understanding what needs to be done. That quick, independent and impulsive Aries will now bring forward the Pisces artistic nature that your intuition told you was always there. It has been difficult for Aries to have patience. Now patience will no longer be an issue, as you grow into your Piscean dreamy, introspective, compassionate realized self. With new understanding and insight, you have the ability not only to start things but also follow them through. This is the Renaissance of Aries.

Aries is the first sign of the Zodiac, and in many old civilizations, it is the beginning of the new year. The spring, the primavera, is the starting of new life as projected so vividly in nature's flowering. Just as nature rushes to bloom, so does the Aries personality, because it is filled with tremendous energy. Now take this burst of energy and put it into Pisces, the last sign in the Zodiac that is filled with wisdom and patience. Pisces has been through all the signs and houses. It is like the great-grandparent and the child. There is a special bond and understanding between the beginning of life and the end.

The AriPiscian has come full circle, pulling together the last sign in the Zodiac with the first one. It takes the watery, mutable, feeling, functioning Piscean traits of sensitivity and deep emotion and blends them with the fiery, cardinal, intuitive function of Aries' traits of actions and willfulness. Thus, AriPiscian comes out with a whole new being. In this new AriPiscian element, the Pisces Fish can live with the Aries Ram. Aries will find a gentler way of life without losing any of the elements of its positive qualities. The Pisces' water slowly washes away any negativity as we evolve to the fourth dimension. Out of this merger will come the birth of an entirely new and different being, one of enlightenment and grace.

Practical Applications. With this new and very different coloring you are acquiring, there will be some adjustments you will need to make to help the transition go smoother. One of the things you can do is be mindful of what you are eating. You should eat tomatoes, for they contain a high quantity of potassium phosphate that Arians tend to lack. The change can be a cause of depression, because the Piscean in you tends to be anemic. Eating raisins, dates and cereals can help restore you. Also, flower essences are very helpful and very simple to make or to buy in most health food stores. To make an essence just put a couple of flowers in a glass of water, place in the sun for a few hours, and then drink the water. Impatiens is the flower for Aries. And as the name suggests, it is the remedy against impatience, irritability, and frustration. Anyone can get into this state of mind, but it is a real Aries trait.

For your new Piscean side, the flower is the Rock Rose; it is the remedy against terror. Pisces tends to get panicky quickly which makes conscious thought and decision next to impossible. This remedy provides calm and courage. Things are changing and sometimes it takes a little help to find balance. Flower remedies work with no negative side effects; don't hesitate to try them. Flower remedies work on the subtle body. The subtle body then heals the physical body. True healing always comes from the subtle body. More and more evidence of this healing will be demonstrated, for Ophiuchus rules the subtle body from the most colorful place in the sky. (See book cover)

AriPiscian

	The Old Aries	**New Aries**
Glyph	Ram's horns	Two fish tied together
Symbol	Ram	Fish
Key Phase	I am	I believe
Key Word	Initiator	Transcendence
Mode	Intuition	Feeling
Element	Fire	Water
Quality	Cardinal	Fixed
Polarity	Yang/Masculine	Yin/Feminine
Ruler	Mars	Neptune
Birth Stone	Diamond	Aquamarine
Healing Stone	Ruby	Amethyst
Anatomy	Head/Face	Feet
House	First	Twelfth
Color	Red	Sea Green
Flower	Sweet Pea	Water Lily
Healing Flower	Impatiens	Rock Rose
Opposite/Attract	Libra	Virgo
Musical Key	A Major	B Minor
Tarot Card	The Emperor	The Moon

Note: You will remain your original sun sign, but now you will also have additional energies and coloring of either a new sign or double your original sign.

41

You Are Transforming: From Taurus to TaurArian and TaurTaurian

April 19 to May 20—The Spirit of Taurus

My Dear TaurArian and TaurTaurian,

There will be about 25 days of Aries that run from April 19th to May 13th. If you were born between May 13th to May 19th, you will remain Taurus, but you will be a double Taurus—a TaurTaurian. Obviously, there is a need for some of the true stability of the Taurus. With dependability and patience to help stabilize the rest of the Zodiac as we go through this transition, you will have the persistence to maintain and thoroughly understand that love is the only one true emotion that we experience. By having that double Venus as your ruling planet, you know the art of sensuality and its importance.

The TaurTaurian is the brick and mortar of human experience. You are able to ground your love for all things; you will understand and experience the highest form of love—unconditional love. The double Taurus will be confident; you will feel the grace and ease of your completeness. You will know self-love; your natural instincts will flourish for the benefit of others.

In your heart, you are the love child of the Zodiac. Experiment with being more tenderhearted and a little less stubborn by working with the added energies you now have. TaurtAurian is gifted and capable of truly effecting the environment with great force, giving the love it needs to undergo the evolution to the fourth dimension. Whether or not you choose to be in the forefront as one of the leaders of the earth, you can achieve the same results within yourself and be influential with anyone who comes into your presence. The energy of the flow of unconditional love that is developing in you will emanate out into the ethers.

TaurArians are those born in the first part of Taurus who will be taking on the Aries energy of being dynamic, independent and active initiators and blending these qualities with their conservative, stable, loyal, dependable and artistic loving ways while being very comfortable living in the movement. It is a real gift that Aries brings you: the ability to concentrate on the present.

Venus and Mars, the ruling planets of Taurus and Aries, are an unbeatable combination. There are many famous paintings of Venus and Mars as well as books written about Venus and Mars. Imagine containing and possessing the energies of these two planets! What a love affair with life! There is perfect balance of the masculine Aries and the feminine Taurus. Aries is bringing you the action and fearlessness that is needed for your pioneering work and the ability to take it where you have never gone before—into the sensuality and flow of the ethers of love in all things. Once you feel that flow—that fire inside—the pure energy of unconditional love will emanate from you. However, the new TaurArian's journey can be at first one of frustrating conflict between having it right now and waiting for the right time. The intuitive Aries and the sensuous Taurus are blended together to teach you and expand your consciousness.

Practical Applications. With this new and very different coloring, there will be some adjustments to be made. To help with this transition, diet is important; celery can help clear the system of over-indulgence (Taureans just love the good life.) With Aires' coloring, Taurarians need to eat tomatoes for potassium, the lack of which can cause depression, the flip side of Aries' exhilaration. Flower essences are also very useful and very easy to make or buy in a health store.

Gentian is the flower essence used for Taurus. It's for the relatively mild downheartedness that is sometimes felt by the Bull. This remedy can be used to lift the spirit. For that new Aries in you, it's the flower called Impatiens for impatience. These remedies act upon the very important part of you, your subtle body (the "subtle body" will be covered in Chapter Four).

TaurArian

	The Old Taurus	**The New Taurus**
Glyph	Bull's head and horns	Ram's horns
Symbol	The Bull	The Ram
Key Phrase	I have	I am
Key Word	Maintain	Initiate
Mode	Sensation	Initiate
Element	Earth	Fire
Quality	Fixed	Cardinal
Polarity	Yin/Feminine	Yang/Masculine
Ruler	Venus	Mars
Birth Stone	Emerald	Diamond
Healing Stone	Rose Quartz	Ruby
Anatomy	Neck/Throat	Head/Face
House	Second	First
Color	Green	Red
Flower	Daisy	Sweet Pea
Healing Flower	Gentian	Impatiens
Opposite/Attract	Scorpio/Ophiuchus	Libra
Musical Key	F Major	A Major
Tarot Card	Hierophant	Emperor

Note: You will remain your original sun sign, but now you will also have additional energies and coloring of either a new sign or double your original sign.

45

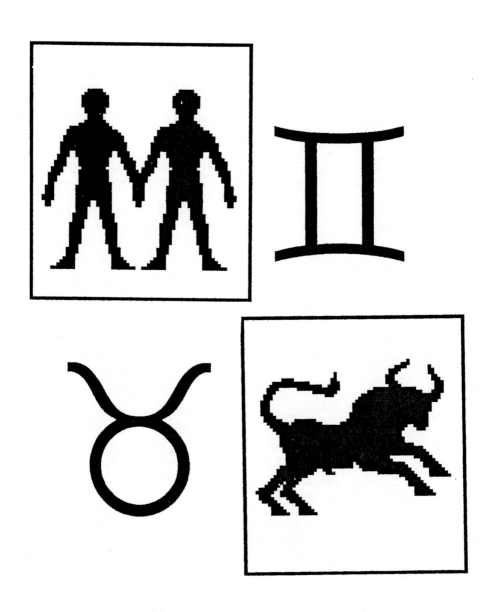

You Are Transforming: From Gemini to GemTaurian

May 20 to June 19—The Vitality of Gemini

My Dear GemTaurian,

Taurus, the Bull, will now be lasting for 37 days. All of Gemini will be included in Taurus. This is not difficult for the versatile Gemini. In fact, this is what at least one of the twins has always yearned for—roots in the earth and a feeling of stability in life. That quick wit and inventiveness of yours is going to pay off in a practical way. The social butterfly that you are will very easily enjoy this dual personality of being able to have the power of endurance, and practicality, as well as the love of luxury and good food. All that intellectualizing and amusing conversation can become warm-hearted and affectionate. This will really make you the center of every party.

This change is needed for the evolution of the planet. You will carry the words of love. Taurus is ruled by Venus, the goddess of love. Gemini is ruled by Mercury, the messenger of the gods. Only a Gemini could spread the words of knowledge so quickly with your great communication skills and intellectual qualities. Now, combined with Taurus' power to love, you surely will be one of the more outspoken and listened to voices of the new age. Your energy will be so prolific that things around you will just speed up.

The energy or force that is now creating The GemTaurian is external and internal. There are times when this will not be a gentle transition; it will be one of enormous changes, both mentally and physically. This shift will change and alter your whole being so greatly that it will seem as if you are a whole new person. You will even talk and look differently. The energies will increase as we move more into the Aquarian Age. Your growth is not only in your new earthly Taurus nature but also in your airy Gemini actions, involving what you think and say. You will be wondering where those words and those prolific ideas came from. You will also be checking the mirror to see if it's still you.

There will be very few dull moments with this combination, and because of the enormous energy flow, be aware of burnout. When your body is on overload, go into your mind and try being that old Gemini and fly above your body. When your mind is ready to explode, go into that

47

body and become a grounded, fixed, sensation loving Taurus. Breathe in the ethers of Ophiuchus slowly and deeply, and trust the process.

Practical Applications. With all this change coming, a little help is needed sometimes just to keep things in balance. Become aware of what you are doing with your body; notice what you eat. Geminians need to eat lettuce and cauliflower to combat lung problems like bronchitis to which they sometimes fall prey. For the new vibration coming in, Taurus needs celery to clear the system of over-indulgence.

Here again, as with the other signs, flower essences are helpful. Cerato is the flower for Geminis and the remedy for lack of faith in their own judgment. Geminis have to contend with a twin; therefore they often second-guess themselves. This flower essence will help ease that confusion. For the Taurian downheartedness that follows when something has gone wrong—Genetian flower remedy is for you.

Things are changing, and change can be upsetting. With a little help to find balance, the flower remedies will be effective. There are no negative side effects to worry about, unlike certain medications prescribed by physicians. The flower essences work on the subtle body. If you have never investigated the power of flower essences and the amazing energy that surrounds the flower, please do so. More information can be found in your health food store—it's worth a look. Remember disease is dis-ease with your own inner core being. To stop dis-ease it is sometimes good to start with a very basic simple awareness of what you are eating and what you are thinking, saying and doing. Then listen to your body and hear what it is telling you.

GemTaurian

	The Old Gemini	**The New Gemini**
Glyph	Roman number II	Bull's head and horns
Symbol	The Twins	The Bull
Key Phrase	I think	I have
Key Word	Question	Maintain
Mode	Thought	Sensation
Element	Air	Earth
Quality	Mutable	Fixed
Polarity	Yang/Masculine	Yin/Feminine
Ruler	Mercury	Venus
Birth Stone	Agate	Emerald
Healing Stone	Alexandrite	Rose Quartz
Anatomy	Shoulder/Arms	Neck /Throat Hands/Lungs
House	Third	Second
Color	Chartreuse	Green
Flower	Lily of the Valley	Daisy
Healing Flower	Cerato	Gentian
Opposite/Attract	Sagittarius	Scorpio/Ophiuchus
Musical Key	G Major	F Major
Tarot Card	The Lovers	Hierophant

Note: You will remain your original sun sign, but now you will also have additional energies and coloring of either a new sign or double your original sign.

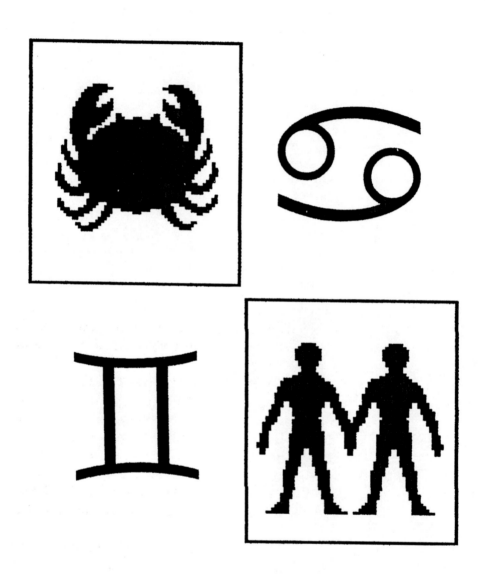

You Are Transforming: From Cancer to CanGemian

June 20 to July 21—The Magic of Cancer

My Dear CanGemian,

Gemini will last about 31 days, from June 20 to July 20. The Crab born on the cusp of Gemini will also be touched with some love from Taurus's Venus. The Crab born at the end of Cancer will be a double Moon, which means you will become very sensitive to the point of being psychic.

Now back to the 28 days in the middle of Cancer. Your coloring will be that of Gemini. What gifts do the twins come bearing for Cancer? They bring adaptability and inventiveness. You will be able to turn every place you go (and you will be going places) into a warm and loving environment just by your appreciation for all that exists. Your intuitiveness and ability to make people feel comfortable will be magnified with the Gemini curiosity and ability to communicate. You will be able to understand and explain the concept that our home is the whole earth/Gaia, and that all things are interconnected. With the new flair you are developing for writing and for language, you will be able to understand and explain the importance of living in harmony with others.

You will be a healer of the new age. You will take that Cancer moon that represents psychic ability and stop being overly traditional and cautious. You will use the psychic connection with Gemini's Mercury to be a hands-on healer. Your touch will be able to heal people suffering with everything from a broken leg to a broken heart. A lot of this new energy is swirling around you in the ethers. Grab hold of it and use it. Let the Merlin in you come out. Gemini's gift to you will be lightness of mind and body and you will make the transition into the Fourth dimension effortless, like a breath of fresh air.

You are just beginning to sense the magical and mystical and the sweet smells that float in the ethers. Your journey commences with a Shakespearean moment: you are able to find the beauty in all things, large and small. Use your magical powers with understanding and with Gemini's gifts to you, you will share them with the world. The CanGemian will find joy in service. You've been the caretaker and the mother. Now you will bring your work to a higher level of understanding and work with the light vibrations in the ethers that Gemini is bringing in. Let yourself blossom into the reality of the healing love energies.

Practical Applications. With the new and strange energies that Cancer is acquiring from Gemini, there will be some adjustment in your life. To help things flow, take special care of your body, beginning with what you eat. Cancerians need foods rich in calcium to prevent cracked skin and poor teeth. Watercress and milk are recommended for Cancerians. Lettuce and cauliflower are necessary for Geminis to combat bronchitis and cold. Also, flower essences are very helpful. The Clematis flower essence is for the Moon Child, whose mind drifts away from the present into fantasies of the future, or into alternative versions of the present. The Clematis remedy is used when you don't feel sufficiently anchored in reality to make things happen. The Gemini's Cerato flower remedy will help in making decisions. Cerato is the remedy for people who lack faith in their own judgment. It helps you to decide upon a course of action and to carry it through.

Too many worries create dis-ease in the body. It is amazing that just a few simple steps can help keep you healthy—the most important aspect is being mindful of all your actions. When you are not on track with what is right for you, your body talks to you. Listen to your body, and observe if there is any dis-ease, anything you are not comfortable with. Find out why, and change it before it changes you. The dis-ease can come from trying to live a lie. Pay more attention to your feelings. Your body simply knows what is right and what is not.

CanGemian

	The Old Cancer	**The New Cancer**
Glyph	Crab's claws	Roman numeral II
Symbol	The Crab	The Twin
Key Phrase	I feel	I think
Key Word	Nurture	Question
Mode	Feeling	Thought
Element	Water	Air
Quality	Cardinal	Mutable
Polarity	Yin/Feminine	Yang/Masculine
Ruler	The Moon	Mercury
Birth Stone	Pearl	Agate
Healing Stone	Moonstone	Alexandrite
Anatomy	Breasts/Stomach	Shoulder/Arms/Lungs
House	Fourth	Third
Color	Cream	Chartreuse
Flower	Water Lily	Lily of the Valley
Healing Flower	Clematis	Cerato
Opposite/Attract	Capricorn	Scorpio/Ophiuchus
Musical Key	E Minor	F Major
Tarot Card	The Chariot	The Lovers

Note: You will remain your original sun sign, but now you will also have additional energies and coloring of either a new sign or double your original sign.

You Are Transforming: From Leo to LeCancian or LeLeo

July 22 to August 22—The Higher Vibration of Leo

My Dear LeoCancian and LeLeo,

From July 20 to August 10, the first 18 days of Leo, the influences of Cancer will be felt. Cancer is ruled by the Moon, and Leo is ruled by the Sun. Leos born August 10 and after become double Leo, from the Lion to the Lion King. You probably already feel your royal creative juices flowing, and your flair for the dramatic is increasing along with your generosity and leadership. Your animal magnetism will attract a variety of people. Being the great romantic that you are, watch that you don't leave a string of broken hearts behind you. Be careful of vanity and of always having to be center stage. It's easy for you to rule. But be aware of your power, for which you will be accountable.

For Leos between July 20 to August 10, Cancer is bringing you the gift of the Moon's intuitiveness and psychic abilities. Take only the best of what Cancer offers—kindness, sensitivity, and a powerful imagination. Mix that with your creativity and leadership, and you have an unbeatable combination. This self-assured lion will be given a good memory and a sympathetic heart.

The Sun deals with the ego and the Moon with the soul. Let your soul shine through and dance in the light. Your life is not about ego. It's about transformation to a higher vibration of the realized self. It's about finding your soul's purpose in this life. It's about having dominion over your body, mind and soul. It's about inner strength. It's about coming from the heart. It's about remembering the power that you possess and the impact it has. Be aware that your every word and action affects your body as well as the vibrations it carries to others around you. Work with these new energies, cultivating self-discipline, but never losing your spontaneity and elegant regal being. Let that combination of fire and water make steam as only as a LeoCancian can. Let that steam blend with the ethers of Ophiuchus to give you that fuel needed to radiate a healing love. For both LeLeian and LeCancian there is a new, even more intense magnetic force around you that will bring faster results for what you wish to happen. Therefore, be very careful what you wish for. It is a lot easier to materialize things now. It may be hard to undo if you decide later that it was not what you really wanted. Just remember, LeoLeon and LeCancian, you are brilliant and glowing when you work from your heart.

Practical Applications. Even Leo may need a little help in this transition to a higher vibration in the body. Watch what you are eating. Plums, peas and oranges should be part of this lion's diet for reducing heart strain, especially for the double Leo. Foods rich in calcium are good for the LeoCancian. Deficiency in calcium does affect the moonchild with dry cracked skin and problems with teeth. Stay on top of this if you want young, youthful-looking skin and beautiful teeth.

Flower essences are also very helpful. The Vervain essence is perfect for the LeoLeian, the perfectionist with a keen sense of justice and extreme mental energy. Your enthusiasm can be infectious and you have a strong need to persuade others, to share your point of view. Sometimes you can get to the point of not listening to alternative viewpoints. This puts you under a great deal of stress, which is hard to switch off. Take this remedy when you feel like you've been on stage too long. It helps you pull back from time to time so that your body and mind can be restored. It encourages the wisdom to enjoy life and the passage of time instead of always having to be "on."

The essence from Clematis is for the LeCancian, whose mind will sometimes drift from the present into fantasies of the future—a great dreamer. This remedy helps to bring you back to earth and back to yourself so that you can build castles in life as well as in the air. With all your dramatic ways, you may also want to have some of Bach Rescue Remedy—a combination of flower essences—around.

LeCancian

	The Old Leo	**The New Leo**
Glyph	Lion's tail	Crab's claws
Symbol	The Lion	The Crab
Key Phrase	I Will	I Feel
Key Word	Dramatic	Nurture
Mode	Intuitive	Feeling
Element	Fire	Water
Quality	Fixed	Cardinal
Polarity	Yang/Masculine	Yin/Feminine
Ruler	The Sun	The Moon
Birth Stone	Ruby	Pearl
Healing Stone	Topaz	Moonstone
Anatomy	Heart	Breasts/Stomach
House	Fifth	Fourth
Color	Gold	Cream
Flower	Marigold	Water Lily
Healing Flower	Vervain	Clematis
Opposite/Attract	Aquarius	Capricorn
Musical Key	E Flat	E Minor
Tarot Card	Strength	The Chariot

Note: You will remain your original sun sign, but now you will also have additional energies and coloring of either a new sign or double your original sign.

57

You Are Transforming: From Virgo to VirLeian and VirVirian

August 22 to September 21—The Beautiful Luminescence of Virgo

My Dear VirLeian and VirVirian,

In the first three weeks of Virgo, until September 15, you will be given the powerful energy of Leo. To explain Virgo, I must go back to the Greek myths. Virgo, the daughter of Jupiter, was the Goddess of Justice. When The Golden Age ended, and men defied her rule, she returned to the heavens in disgust. Now as we go into the Age of Aquarius, you will be working with a feminine energy. The tools given to you by Leo will let you rule again as the Goddess of Justice, not as the blindfolded Justice. This time your analytical, meticulous and modest ways are going to become impressively powerful and creatively magnetic. You have always been very scientific in your fact-finding mission to seek perfection. Now add a little showmanship and drama with your gift from Leo. Everyone will listen to what you have to say. Leo's sun will shine light on Virgo and take you to center stage.

Those of you in the last week of Virgo will become double Virgos. You will take from the best of your sign and stop oscillating between two extremes. You will seek perfection and be perfection without being a perfectionist; there will be beauty in your practicality. You will become non-judgmental; you will know justice but you will not judge. There will be no time to be the critical skeptic, just the seeker of truth, justice and beauty.

With the sun shining so brilliantly on you, Virgoleain, you glow and are luminescent. As the sun shines, you will discover all kinds of wonderful, once-hidden parts and ability. It is as if you are finding yourself. By doing so, you will find new sources of power available to you, accessed by your new sense of identity.

You can effortlessly become clairvoyant. Clairvoyance is just clear seeing. If you can see yourself clearly, then you can see everyone else just as clearly. The sunshine from Leo's fiery aggressive nature will manifest itself in exposing you to yourself. What a gift—to be able to see yourself and others without the mask of ego. There will be no more secrets, not even from yourself. Allow others to share in your joys and sorrows.

This is not an easy transformation, but the rewards are great. The practical earthly element of the sensation function and your analytical thought pattern, blending beautifully with the intuitive function of the creative fires of Leo, aided by the ethers of Ophiuchus, do produce a protective angelic halo effect around you.

Practical Applications. To help illuminate oneself, I think it is important to be aware of what one puts into one's body. Lemons are great for Virgos, either in water or on food. Lemons clean your whole system so you can glow. The Leo part of you needs plums, peas and oranges to prevent your new Lion's heart from being strained. It is so important to be aware that not only is technology changing, so, too, are your body, mind and spirit.

Here again, flower essences are very helpful - don't underestimate "Flower Power." The flower Virgos need to take is Centaury, which is for people who find it difficult to say "no" to others. Virgos are kind, gentle souls, and like to be of help to others. Sometimes other, more ruthless, people will take advantage of them and Virgo becomes the slave to the wishes of others. This flower remedy does not harden your personality; instead, it supports the development of courage. It helps you draw that line and make your own space. For your new Lion side, the Vervain flower essence is for the perfectionist that can arise in you. It allows you to see that life is to be enjoyed and that everything is perfect just the way it is. Don't worry; worry will take your glow away. Vervain will help you find your inner wisdom. The flower essences work on the subtle body. The subtle body is the core of where your healing, wisdom, and energy begins. With Ophiuchus making you aware of your subtle body, you can now learn to work with your it.

VirLeian

	The Old Virgo	**The New Virgo**
Glyph	Greek for virgin	Lion's tail
Symbol	The Virgin	The Lion
Key Phrase	I Analyze	I Will
Key Word	Meticulous	Dramatic
Mode	Sensation	Intuition
Element	Earth	Fire
Quality	Mutable	Fixed
Polarity	Yin/Feminine	Yang/Masculine
Ruler	Mercury	The Sun
Birth Stone	Sapphire	Ruby
Healing Stone	Rhodochrosite	Topaz
Anatomy	Intestines/Gall Bladder	Heart
House	Sixth	Fifth
Color	Indigo	Gold
Flower	Pansy	Sunflower
Healing Flower	Centaury	Vervain
Opposite/Attract	Pisces	Aquarius
Musical Key	C Major	E Flat
Tarot	Hermit	Strength

Note: You will remain your original sun sign, but now you will also have additional energies and coloring of either a new sign or double your original sign.

You Are Transforming: From Libra to LibraVirian

September 22 to October 21—The Beauty of Libra

My Dear LibraVirian,

From September 16 to October 31, there are 45 days of the new Virgo. All of Libra will be feeling the Virgo influence. Libra loves beauty and harmony and pleasant living conditions. Libra's biggest problem is an inability to make decisions. Now, with Virgo in the scheme of things, you will be much more discriminating and analytical. You will analyze situations much more quickly, but you will seek balance in your perfection. You will find yourself becoming more practical in what you do. It will be easier for you to keep your home clean and beautiful.

Libra is ruled by Venus, and Virgo is ruled by Mercury. With Mercury to carry your message—be it writing, painting or some other art form—you will be communicating through the ethers all your pure understanding of beauty and love. This is your mission here on Earth. You feel out of balance unless you have someone with whom to share life. You are the quintessential partner. But first, be your own best friend and see the beauty inside of you.

Beauty is in the eye of the beholder, and Libra has much beauty to behold and also sees the true beauty of things. The analytical, practical and earthy elements of Virgo effortlessly integrate with the airy element and social graces of the Libra, thus making the search for beauty profound. In this pursuit, like a moth to a flame, you are drawn to beauty - in people or in art. You appreciate the beauty of living in harmony with nature and in balance with the universe.

LibraVirians are truly seeking the ideal outward representation of their own inner visions, fueled by a very intensive belief in themselves. A mix of sensations is Virgo's gift to Libra to help him or her identify (i.e., decide) what is needed in any circumstance. Virgo gives Libra its balance.

Libra is surrounded by the energies of Venus and by Virgo's energies from the messenger, Myrciaria. Libra now becomes one of the leaders in this new age by teaching and delivering the message of love and balance. In this search, Libra will know that the physical, as well as the spiritual, must be in harmony with one another.

Practical Applications. For balance in everything, especially in your diet, be mindful of what you are taking into your body. Strawberries are great for Libras; they are high in a mineral salt that helps maintain balance between acids and normal body fluids. For that beautiful Virgo virgin side of you, water with lemons will cleanse and balance your skin. Flower essences are also very helpful; it is amazing how the energy of the flower fuses with the water and, when ingested, makes a noticeable difference in your body. The flower essence Scleranthus is for Libra and it helps to clear your mind.

Libra's indecisiveness commonly affects small as well as the big decisions. For example, should I buy the black hat or the red one? Should I marry Peter or Paul? There may even be mood swings and motion sickness from not being able to make up one's mind. The Scleranthus Flower Remedy helps to make you act more decisively and to know your own mind. For the Virgo in you, Centaury flower remedy helps you to say no - which, after all, is a decision. It supports the development of courage and self-determination and frees you from the desires and commands of others. Flower remedies, eating right or just being aware and mindful of what you are doing will all help you to find your joy.

LibraVirian

	The Old Libra	**The New Libra**
Glyph	The Scales	Greek spelling for Virgin
Symbol	The Balance Scales	The Virgin
Key Phase	I Balance	I analyze
Key Word	Diplomatic	Meticulous
Mode	Thought	Sensation
Element	Air	Earth
Quality	Cardinal	Mutable
Polarity	Yang/Masculine	Yin/Feminine
Ruler	Venus	Mercury
Birth Stone	Opal	Amethyst
Healing Stone	Jade	Rhodochrosite
Anatomy	Kidney/Lower Back	Intestines/Gall bladder
House	Seventh	Sixth
Color	Pink	Indigo
Flower	Rose	Pansy
Healing Flower	Scleranthus	Centaury
Opposite/Attract	Aries	Pisces
Musical Key	A Flat Major	C Major
Tarot Card	Justice	Hermit

Note: You will remain your original sun sign, but now you will also have additional energies and coloring of either a new sign or double your original sign.

You Are Transforming: From Scorpio to ScorVirian or ScorLibrian

October 22 to November 20—The Dramatic Scorpio

My Dear ScorpVirian and ScorpLibrian,

Scorpio has now been split into two signs. The first week of Scorpio, October 22 to October 30, will have the coloring of Virgo. You will be analyzing all your desires. Your intensity will become much more practical and discriminating. All of those powerful feelings and emotions are going to be easier to control: this is your gift from Virgo. Scorpio's element is water, and Virgo's element is earth. When water falls upon the earth, things grow. Your incredible imagination and your sense of purpose will be supported now by the earth. You will find it easier to build structure and bring things to fruition in all areas of your life.

For the ScorpLibrian born between October 31 to November 21, your new coloring will be the beauty and balance from Libra. The passion you have about everything you do will become much more harmonious. That trauma-drama you always seem to have around you will be redefined. Your passion will still be there, but you'll be a little less secretive, more social and more diplomatic. For the earth to raise its vibrations to the next dimension, we must all be able to work together as one. Libra will be a breath of fresh air in your life. Libra will lighten some of that load you carry so you can move quickly into the new realm of the magical garden of the fourth dimension. Now that Scorpio and Ophiuchus are housemates, you are one of the first to feel the effect of Ophiuchus.

Fireworks can be the result of this meeting. To start with, Scorpio's house has been divided up, and all that energy has been compressed into one week (see New Signs Chart). Therefore, what's left of Scorpio has been intensified. Pluto, Scorpio's ruling planet, is the planet of extremes, ongoing changes, turmoil, death, rebirth and intense experience. You know that whatever Pluto touches, changes. Pluto has brought Ophiuchus right into Scorpio, the eighth house.

For the ScorpVirian, this means Virgo's Mercury is bringing you the gift of communication. Mercury is giving you the power to tell the world about your turbulent past, thus freeing you from it. Having this ability to communicate gives you the bliss of the present. It takes you out of the pain of your past and soothes your fears of the future. Is it important for your, and the planet's transformations, that this is processed through you.

ScorpLibrian also includes Libra's Venus with its love, balance and beauty. Pluto is here to transform our awareness of these concepts. It is quite a big job, and it starts with you. I am sure you already have been feeling your ScorpLibrian self. The 1990's focused on redefining relationships we have with others and with the earth. You, ScorpLibrian, are now first to blaze the trail—to show, learn and teach about love and balance in all its new forms for the next millennium.

Practical Applications. To help this transition flow quickly, be aware of what you are taking into your body. Since Scorpios find it difficult to resist rich foods, prunes should be part of your diet. For the ScorVirian, lots of lemons in your drinking water and on your food will clean and clarify your system. For the ScorpLibrian, strawberries will bring balance to you, for strawberries are high in mineral salts that help maintain balance in the body's system. Also flower essences work wonderfully to regulate moods. The flower essence for Scorpio is Chicory to be used when you feel slighted and hurt, or when you are full of love and caring and these feelings are not reciprocated. This remedy will help to bring out your positive side—love given unconditionally and freely. For ScorpLibrian, the flower essence Schleranthus can help you to act more decisively and with a spiritual awareness. The essences of Centaury can help you to say "no," and to set boundaries.

ScorVirian and ScorLibrian

	The Old Scorpio	**The New ScorpioVi/Li**
Glyph	Scorpion's tail and sting	Greek for Virgin/The Scales
Symbol	The Scorpion	The Virgin /The Balance Scales
Key Phase	I Desire	I analyze / I balance
Key Word	Intense	Meticulous / Diplomatic
Mode	Feeling	Sensation / Thought
Element	Water	Earth / Air
Quality	Fixed	Cardinal / Mutable
Polarity	Yin/Feminine	Yin/ Feminine / Yang Masculine
Ruler	Pluto	Mercury / Venus
Birth Stone	Topaz	Amethyst / Opal
Healing Stone	Garnet	Rhodochrosite / Jade
Anatomy	Reproductive Organs	Intestines / Kidney
House	Eight/shared	Sixth / Seventh
Color	Red	Indigo / Pink
Flower	Chrysanthemum	Pansy / Rose
Healing Flower	Chicory	Centaury/Scleranthus
Opposite/Attract	Taurus	Pisces / Aries
Musical Key	D Minor	C Major / A Flat
Tarot Card	Death	Hermit / Justice

Note: You will remain your original sun sign, but now you will also have additional energies and coloring of either a new sign or double your original sign.

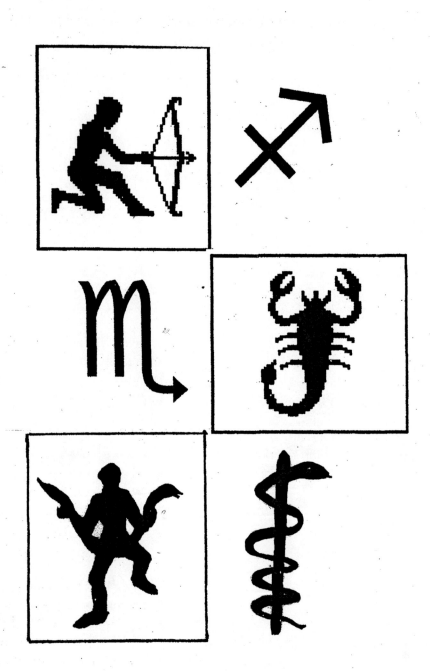

You Are Transforming: From Sagittarius to SagScorpian, Sag Ophiucian or SagSagian

November 21 to December 20—The Transformation of Sagittarius

My Dear SagScorprian, SagOphiucian, and SagSagian,

The first week of Sagittarius will have the flavor and coloring of Scorpio. Scorpio has only six days. The intensity of Scorpio has been condensed into the first week of Sagittarius. You will understand the desire and the intensity of Scorpio. The gift that Scorpio brings to you is passion—a penetrating passion for the unknown. The Sagittarius' fire combines with the Scorpio's water to produce the steam - or energy— necessary for change.

Sagittarians born between November 30 and December 17 are experiencing something very different and new. The Sign Ophiuchus is the physician, the healer, and the one who practices the art. It is because of your powers of visualization, straightforwardness, enthusiasm, broad-mindedness and your philosophical approach to events that you will allow this sign to grow and flourish spreading the knowledge of Ophiuchus. Let the fire of Sagittarius shine on Ophiuchus as it comes out of the dark waters of Scorpio to become the most colorful and beautiful place in the sky (see the cover of the book.)

This is a wondrous gift Ophiuchus has brought to you, for he knows that you will use your talents to fully expand the gifts he offers. Sagittarius' feeling function tunes up to its highest vibration. The body is finely tuned to calibrate every sensation. It tells us when we are tired, hungry, hot, cold, excited, scared—even when we are right or wrong about something. Ophiuchus is now here to show us: 1) How our belief system affects our bodies and our life. 2) What the body is telling us when we have a dis-ease. 3) What we have to do to change.

Sagittarians, born after December 17, will be a double Sagittarius. Sagittarius is a mutable, or flexible, sign, which means that you can morph into something else. The key word for Sagittarius is "Adventure," and the key phrase is "I understand." We have all seen what you can do with your arrows—Sagittarius is famous for that. It's time for your adventures to begin.

71

No matter which Sag you are—SagScorpian, SagOphician or SagSagian—you are the seeker of truth, the constant questioner and the adventurer of the Zodiac. This is why Ophiuchus has come to your sign.

Practical Applications. While on your adventure, it is helpful to be aware of what you are taking into your body. An asparagus and cucumber diet is perfect for you because it's high in silicon, which is needed to promote beautiful skin and hair. For SagScorpian, you'll need prunes to help your digestive system. As for the SagOphician, you will truly need to be aware of your subtle body. Work with your subtle body by doing this exercise: Envision your subtle body around you. Try stepping to the side and separating from your subtle body, first to the right then to left, then forward and back, as if circling around and observing yourself. A lot of healing must take place in the subtle body before it can take place in your physical body. Envision healing the subtle body first, and physical healing will follow.

The flower essences will assist this healing. The Sagittarian's flower is Agrimony. Remember that your archetype is the sad clown, suffering inside but still the life and soul of the party outside. Your friends are the last to know if anything's wrong and they are unaware that you are hiding under a mask of pleasure. The Agrimony essence will help you come to terms with the shadow side of life, enabling you to become a more rounded human being who can laugh at your troubles to *dispel* them, rather than to hide them.

Chicory is used to bring out your positive side and help you give love unconditionally and freely. With your newly found Ophiuchus in your chart, subtle body work and flower remedies will work exceptionally well. Because you have Ophiuchus that represents the subtle body, you may also do well with homeopathic pellets made for the subtle body. They are coded with numbers, the single digit for the physical body, double digits are for subtle body, and triple digits for past life issues. Ask for additional information about homeopathic pellets and flower remedies at your local health food store. The most well known products are the blue tube Boiron pellets and the Bach Flower Remedies.

SagScopian - SagOphician-SagSagian

	The Old Sag	**The New Sags**
Glyph	The Archer's	Arrow Scorpion's tail/Asclepius staff with snake
Symbol	The Archer	Scorpion / Serpent
Key Phase	I Understand	I Desire/ I Heal
Key Words	Expansion	Intense/ Revitalization
Mode	Intuition	Feeling/Feeling
Element	Fire	Water/Ether
Quality	Mutable	Fixed/Fixed
Polarity	Yang/Masculine	Yin/Feminine
Ruler	Jupiter	Pluto/Pluto
Birth Stone	Turquoise	Topaz/Quart Crystal
Healing Stone	Lapis	Garnet/ Salts
Anatomy	Hips/Thighs	Sex organ/Subtle body
House	Ninth	Eight/Eight
Color Royal	Blue	Red/White
Flower	Narcissus	Chrysanthemum/Lily
Healing Flower	Agrimony	Chicory
Opposite/Attract	Gemini	Taurus/Taurus
Musical Key	D Minor	C Sharp
Tarot Card	Temperance	Death/The Magician

Note: You will remain your original sun sign, but now you will also have additional energies and coloring of either a new sign or double your original sign.

You Are Transforming: From Capricorn to CapriSagian

December 21 to January 19—The Oracle Capricorn

My Dear CapriSagian,

Your coloring will be that of Sagittarius, for we know what a perfectionist you are in the traditional, businesslike way. Now that Sagittarius is in your astrological portfolio, you will have vision with your ambition. You will have a better understanding and broad mindedness to expand your cautious, responsible side. The gifts Sagittarius brings to Capricorn are ones of enthusiasm for freedom-loving adventure and a more optimistic way of seeing things. Two of your delightful Capricornian traits are your sense of humor and dry wit. With Sag in your back pocket, you can be generous with yourself and not take yourself too seriously. Sagittarius will allow you to temper your intensity by helping you to understand yourself better. You will be able to show your warm and loving side by opening up your heart, becoming more social, and not just climbing socially for business advancement. Sagittarius is a fire sign: you will use the light of that fire to show the way to a more reliable, practical way of life.

With your unrivaled ability to maintain your focus, your persistent determination to activate a depth of knowledge far beyond other signs, and a new instinctive cognitive ability to know how things work, you're exploding with ideas. Your fiery Sagittarian vision and intuition blend with your down-to-earth, functioning. Capricorn can take aim and shoot your new Sags' arrows to pierce the window of wisdom and look into the future. You have a sense of your physical mortality and vulnerability. Now your vulnerabilities are strengthened with the spiritual insight that Sagittarius and the Ninth house bring (see chart on houses page 93.) This enables you to fully understand life as a continuum. You must rise above third dimension thinking and become a realized individual by expanding your beliefs. You must learn to temper your intensity when you are caught between the expansive influence of Sag's adventurous Jupiter (the ruler of Sagittarius) and the restrictive tendencies of Capricorn's lesson teacher, Saturn (the ruler of Capricorn). Do this by understanding yourself better and not being at the mercy of your moods. Allow your warm and loving side to shine through, especially when you use your knowledge of the power of silence and allow your powers of love to permeate silently in the ethers around you. You are the teacher.

Practical Applications. In order to have all things move peacefully along in your astrological transition, be mindful of what you are eating. Capricornians, when they go to their shadow side, resent change and are reluctant to love, which can cause stiffness in the body. A diet of cabbage and kale will keep such illnesses at bay. Asparagus and cucumber will keep your skin bright and healthy. In this case a flower remedy consisting of water and the petals of Capricorn's Mimulus flower is helpful. Mimulus is the remedy for known fears. Whenever you are frightened, anxious, or if you tend to be nervous and worried about things, the Mimulus flower essence will bring out your quiet courage and strength. For the expansive emotions that will be coming in from the Sagittarius, the Agrimony flower remedy will help when you are feeling low. Don't try to hide your feelings or drown them in drink. When you feel that you must wear a mask to hide your feelings and use jokes, witticisms and smiles to avoid a painful reality, Agrimony will help you to feel at peace. You will not lose your sense of humor, but you will laugh at your troubles to dislodge them rather than laughing to conceal them.

Many people are going through change right now and change is always very uncomfortable at first. If we don't change willingly and gradually with the new vibrations that are coming in, we will change with a cosmic bang (a sudden change experience that our souls create to stop us in our tracks and to draw awareness to something). All of us are changing, some sooner than others, some more dramatically. Change is good. Don't fight it, fear it, resent it or resist it. What you resist will persist. Surrender to it; learn to enjoy watching the changes taking place and the time that's speeding up. Your body and your mind are changing in shape, size and DNA. Enjoy the journey.

CapriSagian

	The Old Capricorn	The New Capricorn
Glyph	Seagoat's horn and tail	The Archer Arrow
Symbol	The Goat	The Archer
Key Phase	I Use	I Understand
Key Word	Structure	Expansion
Mode	Sensation	Intuition
Element	Earth	Fire
Quality	Cardinal	Mutable
Polarity	Yin/Feminine	Yang/Masculine
Ruler	Saturn	Jupiter
Birth Stone	Garnet	Turquoise
Healing Stone	Chrysocolla	Lapis
Anatomy	Knee/Bone/Skin	Hip/Thighs
House	Ten	Ninth
Color	Burnt Umber	Royal blue
Flower	Carnation	Narcissus
Healing Flower	Mimulus	Agimony
Opposite/Attract	Cancer	Gemini
Musical Key	C Minor	B Flat
Tarot Card	Devil	Temperance

Note: You will remain your original sun sign, but now you will also have additional energies and coloring of either a new sign or double your original sign.

You Are Transforming: From Aquarius to AquaCaprian and AquAquarian

January 20 to February 18-The Aquarian Vision

My Dear AquaCaprian, AquAquarian,

I know you know. Aquarius always knows. You have great insight into very unconventional ways of doing things. Capricorn will be there as an influence until February 16th; the last few days of the sign will be double Aquarius. People who are double Aquarians (AquAquarian) will be unique intellectuals with wild imaginations that will create new inroads to help humanity. You are a double Aquarian in the Aquarian Age: trust your vision, your lighting-fast mind, and create greatness.

Capricorn's gift to Aquarius will be ambition with a keen business sense. When I think of Aquarius, I can't help but remember the 1960s and all the changes brought in by the portal we had of the dawning of the Aquarian Age. The portal closed back up by the 1970s, to reopen in 2000. How independent and progressive we were in our thinking, as well as our scientific initiatives, such as "the pill." We went from love-ins to putting a man on the moon. Aquarius is so filled with color—bright, wild, psychedelic color. Now we are adding the muted coloring of Capricorn, transforming the brightness into lovely pastels. The result is a better balanced AquaCap, even with the presence of Aquarius' shadow side. For example, within all that great light and progress of the 1960s, there was also the nightmare of the Vietnam war.

Capricorn is giving you the power to bring your flashes of brilliance into fruition. Aquarians are true humanitarians. With your realized self you will have the energy to bring your progressive ideas for a better future to the planet. You will also be better able to take care of your body, mind and soul—to give yourself the attention and love you have given away to others for so long.

As of the year 2000, we are in the age of Aquarius, and we will be there for another 2,000 years. Slowly, the rest of the planet will be coming around to your way of thinking. You will be energized even more by the gifts Capricorn brings out in you. The ingenious, progressive, unconventional, futuristic ideas that you bring in from the ethers need to be grounded. This now can be done through the practical structure of the sensible earthy energies of Capricorn that you are assuming.

Things will begin to happen to you almost magically and mystically. Your vision, imagination and your kind of knowing in the deepest sense combine to create a universal wisdom within you. Your dreams, visions and unusual experiences are usually vivid and lasting. You have a very active fantasy life, which makes you creative and artistic. You must find an outlet for your creative energy - such as becoming a writer—if you are to find joy. Communicate to others what you experience. Whether it is through art, the spoken word, the written word, or a combination of all three, the world is now ready to listen to you. Appreciate who you are and who you are becoming.

Practical Applications. Aquarius, this is your time; you are the visionary, the seer. But to help things along, pay attention to what you are doing with and take into your body. Eat pomegranates, which contain an alkaline agent in which some Aquarians can be deficient. For the AquaCaprian, cabbage and kale should be part of your diet. It keeps away illness that can cause stiffness in your body.

You have the soul of the original flower child. Speaking of flowers, the double Aquarius flower essence is the Water Violet. Sometimes your independence and self-reliance can make you seem aloof. Your nature is to be quiet and dignified, preferring your own company or that of a few close friends. But when your natural reserve has erected a barrier between you and others, you may actually become lonely. If this happens, this flower remedy can help to bring you back into balance so that you can be more involved with humanity. For the AquaCaprian, the Mimulus remedy is for any new fear of changes. It calms everyday anxieties until you realize that you are safe and that nothing can happen to you without your permission. We create our reality, and we find people and things to mirror back what we have created. Be conscious of what you are creating.

AquaCaprian

	The Old Aquarius	The New Aquarius
Glyph	Waves of electricity	Seagoat's horns and tail
Symbol	The Water	Bearer The Goat
Key Phase	I know	I use
Key word	Unconventional	Structure
Mode	Thought	Sensation
Element	Air	Earth
Quality	Fixed	Cardinal
Polarity	Yang/Masculine	Yin/Feminine
Ruler	Uranus	Saturn
Birth Stone	Amethyst	Garnet
Healing Stone	Aquamarine	Chrysocolla
Anatomy	Ankles/Circulatory System	Knees/Bones
House	Eleventh	Tenth
Color	Purple	Burnt Umber
Flower	Orchid	Carnation
Healing Flower	Water	Violet Mimulus
Opposite/Attract	Leo	Cancer
Musical	Key D	Major C Minor
Tarot Card	The Star	Devil

Note: You will remain your original sun sign, but now you will also have additional energies and coloring of either a new sign or double your original sign.

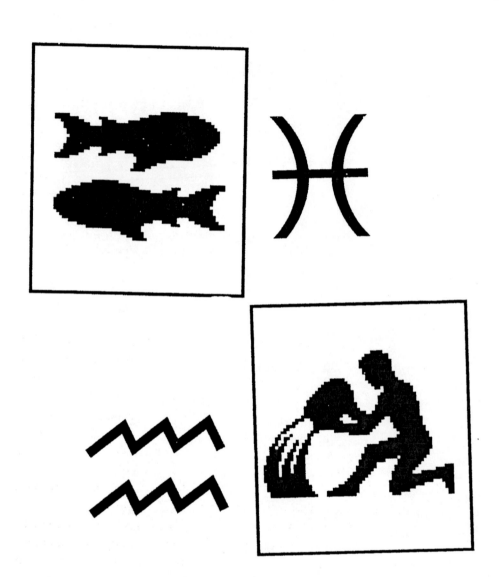

You Are Transforming: From Pisces to PiscAquarian and PiPiscian

February 19 to March 20—The Attunement of Pisces

Dear PiscAquarian and PiscPiscian,

Aquarius will be adding it's coloring to most of Pisces up to about March 12. From March 13th to the 20th, your sign will be double Pisces. Double Pisces are dreamers and artists. Some of you will even practice the art of healing. You have the wisdom of a mahatma, you are an old soul. You find the answer to most of your questions when you go within yourself. You must have art in your life to express yourself. Paint your dream or journal your dreams. Shakespeare was always writing about dreams—discover the mystery of your dreams. Your dreams are filled with information. It is your bridge into the unconscious and into that 90 percent of the unused brain.

The gift that Aquarius brings to Pisces is that of the independent thinker and the freeing of the spirit. Your creative, artistic, dreamy emotions will grow with Aquarius' progressive and intellectual imagination. Aquarius' air and Pisces' water are needed to sustain life. The air can lift the water-forming clouds. Now that Aquarius has freed you from the earth, you can see life from a new, compassionate perspective. You are ready to rain down and feed the planet with your creativity. You will come out of yourself and be a great humanitarian with a big, charitable, Piscean heart. Pisces is ruled by Neptune, the king of the sea. Under the sea all things are hidden; Aquarius is ruled by Uranus, the planet of the unexpected. Pisces will be doing a lot of unexpected things, especially in the realm of spirituality, the occult and the unconscious. You will be having dreams and acquiring much psychic intuition.

PiscAquarians are sensitive souls, and you will have the courage to explore the depth of your soul and learn to soar into the beyond it and into the Fourth dimension. The PiscAquarian craves experiences from the ethers, which fuel your creativity. It's a liberation of feeling, turning your watery element into mist. You can wander back and forth in the two worlds—the water world of Pisces, which is all feeling and emotions, and the Aquarian world of thought and objectivity. You bring the internal subjective to the external objective. The personal and universal - as well as your self-awareness—are always projected out into the world and made into personal and collective reality. Knowing what you want—whether love, a new job or house—first has to be felt inside. As you, true to your sign, have already mastered your inner feelings, Aquarius has made it much easier for you to project what you want or need out into the world and bring it to fruition.

Watch things materialize faster for you now. Remember the Chinese proverb, "Be careful of what you wish for," because for every circumstance in which you find yourself, you must realize that you created it—good or bad. Even if it's not exactly what you thought you were wishing for, it is what you wished; just acknowledge it. Don't blame anyone, especially yourself. Then decide to answer one of the hardest questions in the universe: What do I want to create now?

Practical Applications. With all these new happenings and changes taking place, it's time to become mindful of what you are putting your body through. Pisceans tend to be anemic, and if you're the PiscPiscian, you need to eat raisins, dates and cereals. For the PiscAquarian, you need pomegranates, which contain an alkaline agent. Flower essences also work very well.

For the PiscPiscian, the Rock Rose is the remedy against terror and indecisiveness. Most of the time you don't have this problem. But sometimes with all the changes going on, you can put yourself into a fearful state. The Rock Rose can provide calm and courage; the self is forgotten and strength reappears. The Water Violet essence works when you start to isolate yourself from people. For example, spending too much time on the Internet sometimes contributes to becoming lonely and unable to make close personal contact with others. This flower essence remedy can bring back balance so that you can be involved with the world again.

Change is all around - belief systems are being questioned. Sometimes we may be frightened, but we must learn to enjoy this phenomenally fascinating time. Look at all the exciting changes taking place every day. Don't spend too much time in your dream world. Stay in the present.

PiscAquarian

	The Old Pisces	**The New Pisces**
Glyph	Two fish tied together	Waves of electricity
Symbol	The fish	The Water Bearer
Key Word	I Believe	I Know
Mode	Feeling	Unconventional
Element	Water	Air
Quality	Mutable	Fixed
Polarity	Yin/Feminine	Yang/Masculine
Ruler	Neptune	Uranus
Birth Stone	Aquamarine	Amethyst
Healing Stone	Moonstone	Chyscolla
Anatomy	Feet/Lymphatic System	Circulatory/Circulatory
House	Twelve	Eleventh
Color Sea	Green	Purple
Flower	Water Lily	Orchid
Healing Flower	Rock Rose	Water Violet
Opposite/Attract	Virgo	Cancer
Musical Key	B Minor	D Major
Tarot Card	The Moon	The Star

Note: You will remain your original sun sign, but now you will also have additional energies and coloring of either a new sign or double your original sign.

Claudius Ptolemaeus of Alexandria (120-180AD), the foremost astronomer of his age, author of *Tetrabiblos*, asserted his belief in the physical effects of the planets influences upon earthly things. Ptolemy is shown above in his medieval woodcut measuring the altitude of the Moon.

Part Three
Working with the 13th Sign

Mary Francis Abbamonte

CHAPTER FOUR
The Properties of Ophiuchus

Thus he then classified living creatures into genera and species,
And divided them in every way until he came to their elements,
Which he called the five shapes and bodies
Aether, Fire, Water, Earth and Air
—Xenocrates — On the life of Plato

What are the distinctive features and attributes that Ophiuchus brings to the table of life? He brings back our awareness to the element of Aether. He makes us aware of the fact that air is not just empty space. The air that we breathe in, is filled with everything on the planet that ever was or will be. Our universe is a living organism. Just because, we can't see something in the Third Dimension, doesn't mean it doesn't exist. It is possibly easily seen in the Fourth and Fifth Dimension by the opening of our third eyes. Also, Ophiuchus is about transformation and change, showing us that change is inevitable, while suffering is optional.

The Element of Aether

Ether (from Latin, aether; from Greek, aither) is the "fifth element" and is the element of Ophiuchus. Ether has been misunderstood for a very long time, and among many of the great scientists there have been debates about its very existence. To the Greeks, aether was the rarified air breathed by the gods on Olympus. Aristotle used the term ether for the celestial element—the stuff of the heavens—and said it was subject to different tendencies from the stuff of the earth. Perhaps ether is a vital force such as ch'i, ki, prana, or psychic energy. Newton suggested that ether was responsible for electricity, magnetism, light, radiant heat, and that gravity might be transited by invisible ether.

Much of Albert Einstein's work involved the study of ether and he still did not clearly understand it. In 1920 he gave his lecture on ether and the theory of relativity, stating, "The ether of the general theory of relativity is a medium without mechanical and kinematic properties, but which co-determines mechanical and electromagnetic Events."

89

In 1907. Nikola Tesla, a great scientist, said:

> Long ago man recognized that all perceptible matter comes from a primary substance, or tenuity beyond conception, filling all space, the Akasha or luminiferous **ether**, which is acted upon by giving Prana or creative force, calling into existence, in never ending cycles all things and phenomena.

Please reread the above statement by Tesla, and think about it for a moment. (Nikola Tesla is one of my favorite scientists. He worked with Thomas Edison and had many great accomplishments on his own. His life story is very interesting.)

The existence of ether or aether has always been debatable. Astrologers know, by studying charts and working with people, that aether is that inter-connection between humans that is the energy of the Universe. It is unbounded energy that is matter or intermediate energy, which is electromagnetic or heat energy. Energy never leaves the aethers. Once something is said or done, it is there for all time in the ethers.

Ophiuchus is bringing in the element of aether. For as we move into the age of Aquarius and the Fourth and Fifth dimensions, we will become much more aware of our inter-connectedness and the aether that carries all of our thoughts and actions. Therefore, it is very important that we become mindful of our thoughts and actions, for they will affect the Universe. In the Fourth dimension, the energies will become lighter and will materialize more quickly in form.

If you are carrying the energies of anger or hate, they will materialize around you and in you and thus form a karma that will magnify anger and hate. Make sure this is not what you are creating; become aware of bringing love and beauty into your life. Karma used to take a lifetime to come back. Now, I see that sometimes it comes back very quickly— almost instantaneously. Ophiuchus is here with the element of aether to bring this to your attention and to show you that this is how we get sick. If we are filled with love, compassion and understanding, then this is what our universe will exhibit. Our bodies will become healthier because of it.

Before the Quantum Field there was the "Ether." In the Quantum Field or the Aether field physical energy is all around us. Theoretically, energies can be drawn from the unfilled field. Ether technology is back. This technology will help us affect change in our consciousness similar to the gods of ancient times. Here is one of the messages of Ophiuchus being brought through the aethers: *Bring in the aethers of change-to transcend to the realized self.*

The Glyph of Ophiuchus

The Staff of Asclepius (Greek) Aesculapius (Latin), with a snake coiling around a rod, is well known in today's medicine. Because of the myth of Ophiuchus, and the snake's ability to cast off its skin and regenerate, the snake has become the symbol of healing.

This symbol is often confused with the caduceus of Mercury, which is a doubly-winged wand entwined by two snakes; this is the symbol of the messenger, and not of the physician. Nor should this symbol be confused with the dollar sign. In Greek mythology, Aesculapius, when struck with a thunderbolt from Zeus, was then placed in the sky. After that Aesculapius was called Ophiuchus, which, in Greek, means "serpent holder." Aesculapius is always depicted holding a staff with a snake.

The House of Ophiuchus

Since the measuring device has been constructed by the Observer... We have to remember that what we observe is not nature in itself but nature exposed to our method of questioning.
—Werner Heisenberg

The 13th Sign of Ophiuchus will not move into a thirteenth house. It is moving in with Scorpio, making it a two-family house in the Eighth House. Ophiuchus is raising us up to a higher level of consciousness rather than spreading us out. Ophiuchus has come to work with and expand upon Eighth House issues, such as crisis, emergency and extreme circumstances. It deals with the agony and the ecstasy of life and death.

This House holds information on transformation, rebirth, the personal unconscious, surgeries, injury, psychotherapy, and the way we regenerate and rejuvenate after loss. The House also holds our attitudes toward death, life after death, life as a continuum, ESP, and out-of-body experiences. It has to do with fate and important past-life events that affect us, or the understanding of past life karma. The Eighth House is also concerned with these subtle energy forces that are internal causes of physical manifestations. Or better put:

> *That which we do not confront in ourselves,*
> *we will meet as fate.*
> —C.G. Jung

The Eighth House deals with subjects most of us are uncomfortable talking about, including sex, money and death. You might wonder what Ophiuchus has to do with sex. Ophiuchus has a lot to do with that wonder drug Viagra. It was developed right after Pluto went into Ophiuchus.

The Eighth House also deals with the occult and aspects of science such as higher mathematics and atomic physics. Ophiuchus will countenance the communication with people who are not in these physical incarnations by opening the Third Eye and going beyond the five physical senses.

The Eighth House also deals with "The Occult," which in Ophiuchus' time, (Asclepius' time), was called "the Art." Physicians then worked with astrology, astronomy and herbs. They took care of the whole body, not just a small part of the body as allopathic doctors do today. The specialist has hurt the medical profession more than he or she has helped it. You cannot just take care of a three-inch section of a person's body, as specialists do. You must treat the entire person, including the subtle body. Ophiuchus is here to emphasize this holistic approach to healing.

The Eighth House also deals with OPM, or "other people's money." This is the part that Scorpio (remember, Ophiuchus has moved in with

Scorpio) will control. Scorpios can deal with finances, and they have all the power that money can bring. Scorpio loves to handle people's resources, values, talents, possessions, as well as anything to do with money and finance, stock markets, legacies, inherited money or properties, business partners, corporate money, insurance companies, big business, the IRS, taxes and crime.

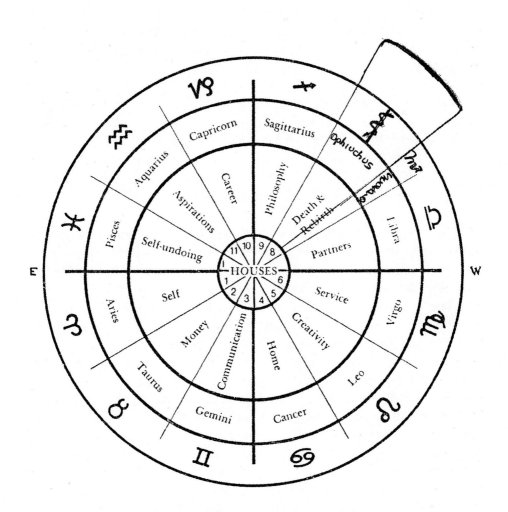

Ophiuchus and Scorpio

Ophiuchus is the teacher of healing and wholeness. What is it doing with Scorpio? For the reader unfamiliar with Scorpio, you must first realize the power of the myth of Scorpio. There is always the raised eyebrow reaction when someone mentions that he or she is a Scorpio (Scorpio deals with all the things impolite and politically incorrect). Scorpio deals with our deepest passions, desires, sexuality, money, fear of the unknown, death and immortality.

We all have to deal with Scorpio at some time in our lives. All the planets eventually travel through all the signs, Scorpio included. And, as was discussed in Chapter 3 and 5, they create aspects with each other. This is not just about a few people born in November.

As C.G. Jung would put it, Scorpio touches our "shadow side." Death comes to us all. Scorpio, being a fixed sign, teaches us about transformation. You would think that this is the job of a mutable sign, but it's not. Scorpio has taught us about death. Now Ophiuchus is here to teach us about rebirth and life as a continuum. We do not escape ourselves in physical death. Until we understand death, we will never understand life.

Shakespeare explores this subject in *King Lear*. The King is facing death. When he finally accepts his physical mortality, Lear transcends the limitations of earthly time. After severing his ego-self, his realized self then steps into the timeless world of immortality.

Many of us who have been "at death's door" have literally stood in the doorway, peered through and returned to tell that the glimpse of the beyond opened up a wellspring of spiritual awareness. In addition, those of us who have lost someone dear to us have also had our spirits opened to new understandings. Ophiuchus has come to open that doorway for us to understand and to rise out of bodies trapped in this earthly plane, thereby freeing our spirits and enabling us to live in two worlds at the same time.

Therefore, sensitive issues or situations with which we don't want to deal, we assign to Scorpio. We call them dark, and they belong to Scorpio. Traditional astrology provides Scorpio with three symbols - the scorpion, the eagle, the phoenix—while all other signs have one. When you talk about not being sure what this sign is about and being afraid to deal with certain issues, these multiple images can confuse anyone. Pluto, the ruler of Scorpio was discovered in the 1930's.

94

The power and energies allotted to the sign of Scorpio are the energy of money and the power that money can give, and take away. It ranges from the sting of the scorpion, to the eagle that has the power to seize unsuspecting prey. It soars above worldly difficulties, to the phoenix that rises from the ashes.

Ophiuchus has come to share this House to bring light and new life into the shadows of complexity by showing our opening of the Third Eye.

The Third Eye

Each sign in the Zodiac has a special relationship to a specific area of the body; Ophiuchus has that relationship with the Third Eye and the Subtle Body.

For readers who are not sure of what and where the Third Eye is, we have two physical eyes in our head from which we see, and a third "eye" from which we perceive. Some say the third eye is not physiologically in one's body. It is a metaphor, and it is symbolically located in the center of the forehead. I believe that it is real, and that it can be opened and will become active when we start becoming our realized self. (The Hindus sometimes wear a red dot in the center of their forehead to symbolize the Third Eye.)

Jesus talked to his disciples about the Third Eye, saying, "If you become of one eye, then you will know my Kingdom of God. If you attain one eye, then all bliss be yours and all benediction."

The Third Eye is not activated in the physical body in the third dimension; it is only in our subtle body. When we move back into the fourth dimension, it will become activated again. With the Third Eye functioning, you can enter different dimensions. With the Third Eye, you can "see" things that are invisible to the physical eye. With the Third Eye functioning, you can look at people and you can see their souls, their spirits, and their realized selves.

The Third Eye represents consciousness. The two physical eyes see only that which a small portion of our asleep brain sees (as was discussed in Chapter Two, we only use a very small portion of our brains; it's as if we are asleep). We are living in a Fourth Dimension world with Third Dimension vibrations. As we transcend into the fourth and fifth vibrational dimensions, we will awaken to full consciousness and awareness of our Subtle Body, which contains the third eye. By seeing with our Third Eye, we will be using more of our brains.

We must remember we are spirits who only temporarily occupy our physical bodies to participate in physical reality. We must also remember that we have physical and non-physical senses. The third eye is one of our non-physical senses. The more we use it, the stronger it gets. I believe that every one of us has had third-eye experiences, but most of us do not pay attention to them or we rationalize them to be something else because of our belief system.

Third Eye Exercises. First you must acknowledge-or at least be open to the idea—that you have a third eye. The Hindus wear a red dot in the center of their foreheads to remind them of their third eye. I am not asking you to wear a red dot. Instead, rub the center of your forehead, thinking while you rub that you are opening your third eye. Do this a few times a day. The third eye is open through the heart. That is why Catholics bless themselves first at the third eye and then the heart. The Third Eye Chakra color is purple or indigo. Envision purple light swirling around your third eye. (For those of you who don't know the chakra system, "chakra" is Sanskirt for wheel or disk and signifies one of seven basic energy centers in the body. Each of these centers correlates to major nerves branching from the spinal column. In addition, chakras correlate to levels of consciousness, archetypal elements, developmental stage of life, color, sounds, body functions and much, much more. The Third Eye is the sixth chakra. This chakra is externalized as the pituitary gland.)

Remember your third eye is open, but you block it by a belief system that denies it. The third eye can also be blocked by shutting down the heart chakra. The heart chakra is the fourth chakra. It is externalized as the thymus gland. This is the center through which we feel love; it is the color green.

How are you in the love department? Do you love yourself? Do you see love in everyone and everything? You don't have to love everyone, but you do have to find the love in them. If you can't find it, look for it. Remember, everyone you meet or come in contact with is your mirror or some part of you, reflecting back to you. Once you understand, accept and integrate this concept into your life, you will heal and find love all around you. You came to this planet to learn love and all its expressions.

It all comes back to love, to activate the heart chakra and the thymus gland (center of your chest). With your fist, pound on the thymus gland thirty times a day. It symbolizes the awakening and also activates and strengthens the immune system. While you are doing this, think about opening your heart, healing yourself and circulating light from your Third Eye down to your heart and back to your Third Eye. The opening of the Third Eye is seeing with your heart; it's seeing the big picture, the complete picture. This is a very different view from allowing your ego to rule (seeing only with your two physical eyes) while you edit out your god self by not seeing with the Third Eye. Your ego has a belief system base that is lacking and acts accordingly. Your god self knows you create your reality and act accordingly. Your god self sees through your Third Eye.

One last exercise: Every time you have a dollar bill in your hand, look at the symbol of the all seeing third eye on top of the pyramid. Let it remind you of opening your Third Eye!

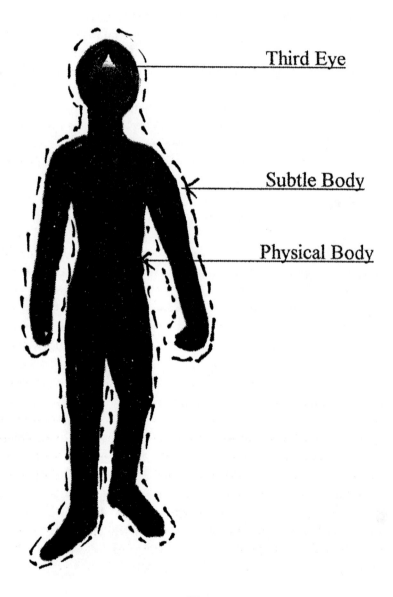

The Subtle Body

Ophiuchus is associated with the Subtle Body. The Subtle Body is sometimes referred to as the Astral Body because it is capable of separating from the physical body in astral projection into the ethers. We all have a Subtle Body. Our Subtle Body vibrates faster than our physical body; therefore, we can't see it in the third dimension. It looks similar to our physical body when it is perceived clairvoyantly or when we slip into the fourth dimension, which happens when we have our psychic moments. The earth is a fourth dimensional plane, and we are now working it in a third dimensional mind. However, we are quickly changing and awakening to the fourth dimension. We are seeing many changes right now in our lives because of this phenomenon.

The Subtle Body (see fig.) is an esoteric substance interpenetrating the physical body and expanding outward about five to eight inches. The Subtle Body is influenced by physical existence. The physical body, in turn, contributes to the physical existence.

The Subtle Body carries all our karma-good and bad—in this lifetime and from our past lives. This karma does affect the physical body. In the fourth dimension of which we are becoming more aware, we are capable of seeing our Subtle Body and working with it in order to help our physical body. In any good health food store, you will find homeopathic medicines that work on your Subtle Body. I believe that in order to heal, one must heal the Subtle Body first. Thanks to Ophiuchus, we are becoming aware of this radical change; we are upgrading our brains as we would our computers. To upgrade our brains, we need to be mindful and be present. Our vibrational rate is speeding up - enjoy the change! Don't fear it! Ophiuchus is not doing anything to us. Ophiuchus is showing us that it is happening.

Subtle Body Exercises. Below are exercises and meditations you can do to help this transitional period to flow smoothly. Just by acknowledging that this is happening, things will speed up and flow painlessly.*(Note: The best way to follow these exercises is to tape record this section and play it back as you do the exercises.)*

Exercise 1. Stand tall, with your arms at your sides. Take a few deep breaths. Feel present in your body. Feel your feet on the ground, your hands at your sides, shoulders back and your head held high. Take a deep breath as you step forward on your left foot, then exhale changing your weight as you rock back on your right foot. Again, take a deep breath, shifting your weight forward on your left foot. Exhale slowly and rock back on your right foot. Put your two feet together. Feel your body and your subtle body moving together as you step forward on the left foot. Rock back on the right. Again, breathe in deeply, be aware of your subtle body, and now shift your weight forward on your left foot. Exhale and rock back on your right foot; put your two feet together. This time as you breathe in, you will step forward *without* your subtle body. Your subtle body will remain still; exhale and move back into your subtle body. Again, breathe in and feel the separation of your body from your subtle body as you step forward. Breathe out and rock back on your right foot. Feel your subtle and physical bodies coming together. Put your two feet together.

Breathe in; let your subtle body step forward while your physical body remains still. Breathe out, and move your subtle body back into your physical body. Again, breathe in and let your subtle body step forward. Feel the separation of subtle body leaving your physical body. It may help if you shut your eyes or fix your eyes on something in the distance. Exhaling slowly, move your subtle body back into your physical body. Feel your subtle body coming back into your physical body. Put your two feet together.

Breathe in as you step forward on the right foot. With your two bodies together, breathe out as you rock back on your left, bringing your two feet together. Again forward on the right foot inhaling, exhaling rock back on the left, bring your two feet together.

Again, this time as you are breathing in, your subtle body will remain still and feel the separation of your physical body from your subtle body. Exhale and move back into your subtle body. Bring your two feet and your two bodies together.

Step forward on the left foot breathing in. This time, step back on the left foot breathing out. You are stepping back, not rocking back, your left foot is behind you. Now bring your two feet together. Again, step forward on the left foot breathing in slowly, step back on your left foot breathing out. Bring your feet together and your bodies together. Step backward on the left foot; your subtle body will be still as your physical body is stepping backward. Feel your two bodies dividing as you breathe in and you are expanding. Breathe out and feel your bodies merging together as you step forward into your body. Again step back, separating from your subtle body, step forward, merging into your subtle body.

This time step back while your subtle body will step forward. There is a bigger distance now between you and your subtle body. Inhale deeply expanding the distance of your two bodies and exhale contracting the distance between your two bodies as you step back.

Now, take three steps back while your subtle body is taking three steps forward. Feel your expansion, envision the separation. Now take three steps forward, your subtle body is stepping back. Feel, sense, experience, the blending, the mix, the unity of the two bodies coming together again.

Now, take, three steps back, inhaling slowly while your subtle body is taking three steps forward. Exhale slowly and with your physical body taking six steps forward. Your subtle body is moving back. Feel your subtle body flow right through your physical body. Experience the feeling and sense while your subtle body is moving right through your physical body. Take three steps back with your physical body as your subtle body is moving forward and you are together again.

Let's do that again; take three steps back with the physical body, while you're visualizing three steps forward with the subtle body. Take six steps forward with the physical body, while you're visualizing six steps back with the subtle body, stepping right through each other. Notice the feeling of your subtle body passing through your physical body. Take three steps back with the physical and visualize the forward movement with the subtle to your starting point. Put your two feet together and two bodies together, as you breathe slowly.

Repeat these exercises on the right foot first then repeat the same exercises going to the left side then to the right side again. Do not ever completely isolate yourself from your body. Don't lose your focus; pay attention to your two bodies. You can send your subtle body anywhere you want, but always envision being attached to it by a silver cord or seeing it with your third eye. You can send your body halfway around the world - maybe not in the first week of these exercises, but with practice. There are some sages, like Sai Baba, who can be in more than one place at the same time, using a method similar to this.

Exercise 2. Envision your subtle body standing in front of you. You are face to face. Look at your subtle body. What do you see? Is it larger than you? Is it strong? Is it healthy? Ask your subtle body if it needs anything from you. Listen for the answer. Is everything OK? Do you need

101

to change something? Is it free from any illness or dark spots? If you see any dark spots in your subtle body send light, energy and love to those spots until they start to lighten. It may take several attempts to lighten an area at first. See light, energies and love flowing from you to your subtle body.

Now change places with your subtle body and look through the eye of your subtle body and see yourself. What do you see? Know that your subtle body loves you, and wants to help you. It can help you with anything you need. Now is the time to see that you can do what you always said you want to do. Through the Third Eye of your subtle body you see that you can create your own reality. You can also see what you are creating, as well as how you can change it. You are able to heal anything in your body.

Scan your body and see your aura. Is it bright? Is it dull? Are there any dark spots? Send light from your subtle body to your physical body to heal any dark spot. Envision what you want, and see your subtle body doing it. Soon your physical body will follow, whether it is healing, dancing or walking on water. Acknowledge your subtle body; make it your best friend. You will be amazed at how much you can accomplish working with your subtle body, as though you were partners.

This could also be explained as being "in the zone." You envision your subtle body doing something, whatever it may be, such as hitting a golf ball into a hole, or dancing a beautiful ballet. The subtle body will take over and support the physical body. Whether you are learning to play the piano or trying to lose weight, your subtle body can be a great source of energy, light, love and knowledge.

CHAPTER FIVE
Transiting Through Ophiuchus

Whatever is born or done this moment,
has the qualities of this moment of time.
—Carl Gustav Jung

A transiting planet is the actual passage of a planet through the different Signs in the Zodiac.

The planets travel at different speeds around the sun so that the time they spend in each of the thirteen signs can vary from two days, as the earth's moon does, to thirty years, as Pluto does. The Moon will pass through Ophiuchus every month while it may take Pluto up to 248 years to make it back into Ophiuchus. Of course, the Sun comes by once a year just as your birthday does. And once a year, Ophiuchus will have the sun transiting through it.

Check how Ophiuchus affects your Natal Chart, your Return Chart, and your Progressed Chart in order to make new charts from the new position of the planets. (Refer to the back of the book for a list of websites to help you find the locations of the planets).

You will be very surprised to see just how much Ophiuchus is now affecting you and the world around you, regardless of your sun sign. The aspects that Ophiuchus is making to other planets and to your sun are very significant, having a special impact as it passes through each sign. This will give you a more precise reading of your individual horoscope. We are undergoing an evolution and so must our astrological charts. (To figure out exactly when the transits occur, either you can use the free web sites listed in the back of the book or refer to the astronomical *Ephemeris*.)

To everything there is a season, and a time to every
purpose under the heaven:
-Ecclesiastes

Aim point RA: 16h 51m Dcc: -12°21'26"
Tue 2001 Dec 11 0:15 UTC
http://www.fourmilab.ch/cgi-bin/uncgilYourtel

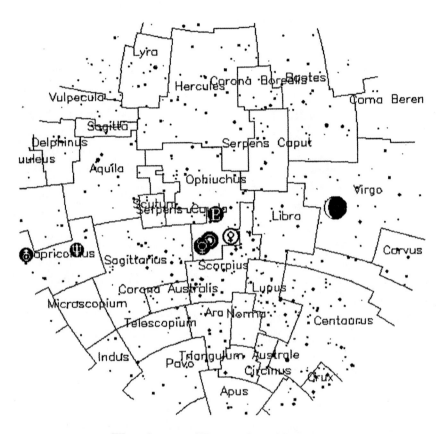

The sky as of December 12, 2001

Note: The Location of The Sun, Pluto Venus, and Mercury.
  all in Ophiuchus. The Moon is in Virgo and Neptune is in
  Capricorn. There are no planets in Sagittarius.

(Note: There are 13 Moons a year, and now there are 13 signs.)

Moon Transiting Ophiuchus

Glyph: Moon in the first quarter
Transiting Time: About One Day
Appearance time: Once a month
Keyword: Nurturing
Key Phrase: Acute awareness of the body
Association with The Body and Mind: Birth, the digestive system, stomach, breast, the sympathetic nervous system, body fluids, emotional disturbance, response, memory, the Third Eye and Subtle Body.

When the Moon is transiting Ophiuchus, it just may be the day you check your calendar to confirm when your last checkup took place or when the dog last saw the veterinarian. You may have an urge to start a diet or to exercise. You will become aware of your needs, both mental and physical. Today you might check in with your family or with yourself just to see how your soul is doing. A new moon in Ophiuchus could open up your psychic awareness. A full moon in Ophiuchus should shine some healing light, taking away any misconceptions you may have. You might have started reading this book when the moon was in Ophiuchus, bringing attention to the moon, your body and the planet at this time. You will also hear about new medical findings, new inroads into human genetics, new drugs and new ways of healing. If you have to go to the doctor, he will be free in his thoughts. He may suggest alternative ideas from a traditional

105

approach to medicine. He may even suggest herbs, positive affirmations, listening to music or just a good walk outside in nature to cure all that ails you. This is a good time to put into the ethers anything dealing with the advancement of your well being.

Mercury Transiting Ophiuchus

Glyph: The winged hat of the god Mercury
Transiting Time: About 17 Days
Appearance: About once a year
Keywords: Health Conscious
Key Phrase: Communication on a visionary level
Association with The Body and Mind: The brain, the intellect, coordination of the nervous system, the respiratory system, mental perception, the thyroid, The Third Eye and Subtle Body.

When Mercury is in Ophiuchus, you understand how important it is to laugh and be happy. You feel a chemical change in your body when you are not happy. You often experience intuitive flashes of great insight. You may enjoy talking about the occult and philosophizing about different aspects of the healing arts. You may love to investigate or probe into the depth of the unknown because of your interest in spirituality.

Whether you write it, talk it, or just try it, there will be no getting away from the fact that with Mercury in Ophiuchus, you will want to be the one leading the pack, being a leader, making new inroads into health or health care reform. You must remember that your perceptiveness can lead you to

107

critically interrogate others. You will see things accurately but not necessarily charitably.

Therefore, before you say exactly what you feel, know not only the importance of your words, but the powerful impact they can have on other people. Your words should not only be accurate but filled with healing love. The keyword is healing.

Venus Transiting Ophiuchus

Glyph: The mirror of vanity of the goddess Venus
Transiting Time: About 18 days
Appearance: Every 224-225 days
Keywords: Healing Love
Key Phrase: How we respond to life affects our bodies
Association with The Body and Mind: Feelings in the body, the lumbar region, throat, kidneys, parathyroid, the power of love, The Third Eye and The Subtle Body

Venus (the planet of love) in Ophiuchus provides you with the ability to know not only the healing aspects of love but also the destructiveness that can occur from a lack of love. Your visionary insight tells you to just keep smiling, and things will get better. In fact, just a smile and a light, humorous, outgoing, friendly, freedom-loving attitude can make everyone feel better. You are also perceptive enough to know that any phoniness with a fake smile of pretense can be deadly.

The stuffing of emotions will surface later as dis-ease in the body. You will learn to release and transcend, move on with love and not get caught in that limitation. You love the outdoors and are often drawn to places of great beauty around the world, finding them therapeutic.

Even with your deep emotions and strong philosophical views, you will always to come back to the fact that all you need is love to heal yourself and the world. With Venus, you come to understand that love is the only emotion there is. Without love, there is fear. Anger is then derived from fear and so a number of negative emotions emerge.. Live in love, in a body of beauty and health, or live in fear and anger with dis-ease and ugliness. You will come to realize that the choice is yours.

The Sun Transiting Ophiuchus

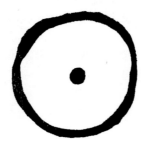

Glyph: The circle of infinity (the dot represents the person within)
Transiting Time: About 18 days
Appearance: Once a year
Keywords: Enlightening
Key Phrase: Shine your light on The Shadow
Association with The Body and Mind: The heart, spine, creative expression, the ego, the Third Eye and the Subtle body.

When the Sun is transiting Ophiuchus, you can't help but somehow get involved in the deeper mysteries of life. The intuitive mind is working in high gear. The Sun is all about ego. The e.g.o. becomes full-blown when you Edit-God-Out. In Ophiuchus, you will transcend outer material circumstances in order to experience a deep level of spiritual reality. The ego will step aside for the awareness of the consciousness of the realized self. If you've ever wished for a sign that God exists, it will be shown now. If you've ever wanted to know what the meaning of life is, the answer will come now. The veil between the two worlds will be thinnest with the sun transiting Ophiuchus. Let your sun shine the light into the valley of the shadow of death, and you will fear no evil. You will understand life as a continuum. All you have to do is listen, and the answer will be there for you.

It is also a good time to investigate or work with different healing arts. If you have been sick, you could have a miraculous cure. If you have been restless, this could become a quiet and peaceful time. If you have felt unloved, you will find the ability to really love yourself and enjoy your own company. Soon you will have materialized just what you need. Ophiuchus will make us look at ourselves in the relationship of the whole

- or to God - and to the oneness of all Force. It awakens something within our soul-self, bringing to us a full realization of the part we must play in the future cycles of manifestation. Now is the time we must open that door to a new vision. It is a great time to burn away our old beliefs about disease.

To realize that which we believe to be true, we prove to ourselves to be true especially within our bodies. You are the center of the universe, not the sun. There is only one universe and that is yours. As Deepak Chopra says, "You are the living center around which every event happens."

Mars Transiting Ophiuchus

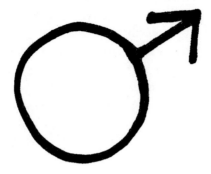

Glyphs: The god of war, Mars; shield and spear
Transiting Time: About One Month
Appearance: Approximately once every two years
Keywords: The Trigger
Key Phrase: Where the action is
Association with the Body and Mind: the muscular and urogenital systems, gonads, adrenal glands, red blood corpuscles, kidneys, cuts and burns, accidents, the Third Eye and the Subtle Body

With great enthusiasm and energy, you're out to heal the world with all the new ideas you have. You are very philosophical about your new insights into the workings of the universe. Nothing makes you happier than a righteous debate or spirited discussion on the "why" of life. You are always on the cutting edge of new things. Sometimes your strong sexual urges can take you to profoundly intense intimacy, with an epiphany of spirituality that you find revitalizing and regenerative to your immune system. Full of action and passion, you find is it difficult to separate your energy from enthusiasm when you embrace a new idea. With Ophiuchus, you will have lots of new ideas. With the opening of your Third Eye and Mars acting as the catalyst (the action verb for Ophiuchus), you will be launched into the fourth dimension. You will find your self one day wanting to start a crusade and the next day being very satisfied with the way things are. Enjoy the knowledge coming in. Learn, feel the joy and don't be fighting Don Quixote's windmills or indulging in the indecision of Hamlet. Fasten your seatbelts and open your mind.

Mars, being the Roman god of war, is about handling your anger, and handling it wisely. When Mars is transiting Ophiuchus, you will become aware what anger can do to your body. There are two kinds of anger, healthy and unhealthy. Unhealthy anger causes disease in the body. Being angry can be so destructive. Now is the time to get over it. A time to move on, a time to forgive, a time to forget, a time to heal. By doing so, you will find time to love and be loved. Mars, in Ophiuchus also deals with passion and action. Let that Mars, excite your love of life. You will probably have some good healthy sex during this transit.

Jupiter Transiting Ophiuchus

Glyph: first letter (in Greek) spelling the god Zeus
Transiting Time: About 7 months
Appearance: About once every 12 years
Keywords: Expanding your consciousness
Key Phrase: Seeing the bigger picture, life's continuum
Association with The Body and Mind: The liver, thighs, hips, master gland or the pituitary gland, the Third Eye and Subtle Body

You're flamboyant and larger than life, but always tasteful and dignified. You have magnetic healing powers that attract people as well as animals. Your greatest joy in life is carrying the light. Somehow you never miss an opportunity to seize the day. Something is always mystical and magical about your optimistic and outgoing beliefs and standards. You travel far, be it worldwide or deep into your psyche, to find your joy, your answers.

While you are a people person and love being the well-dressed center of any party, you are still observing others in order to gain insights into them. When Jupiter is in Ophiuchus, you can almost tell why people do the things that they do. With Jupiter in Ophiuchus, your conscience, your perception, your clairvoyance, and your awareness will enlarge. You will know why one person got sick, and why another didn't. You will know why one walked away from an accident and another didn't. You will see yourself expanding in order to reach your realized self. Your deep insight into people will astound and amaze even you. Luck is with you now; you can find the keys to unlock your unconscious and be able to tap into the universal consciousness for your answers. With Jupiter in Ophiuchus, there will be a light to show you the path back into that large unused portion of your brain. That is the part of us that knows the truth of our being.

Saturn Transiting Ophiuchus

Glyph: Chronos, the god of time; sickle
Transiting Time: About 2 years
Appearance: About once every 28-30 years
Keyword: Learning
Key Phrase: Subtle teaching, major lessons
Association with The Body and Mind: Bones, including teeth, the skin covering the knee, auditory organs, the third Eye and the Subtle Body

When Saturn is transiting Ophiuchus, the slender line between the occult and spirituality disappears. You search for the truth and demand much of yourself. You have excellent powers of concentration and tremendous willpower. Full of energy and intensity, you are focused on seeking wisdom. Much of your wisdom comes through lessons learned. Saturn is the taskmaster of the Zodiac. And in Ophiuchus you will see over and over again this lesson: What you put out will always come back. You will learn that every action has a reaction. And that reaction is felt in the body, either negatively or positively. Saturn will bring to your attention the reason for every ache, pain, sickness, joy, and rush or lack of energy.

No one likes to learn from a taskmaster, but you don't have to let Saturn turn into one. Learn these lessons quickly and with great excitement for they will give you much needed power over all your actions and the ability to respond to life with fuller understanding. When Saturn is finished with you in Ophiuchus, you will be the physician that can heal himself. Use this time wisely because there is much to be gained. By the time Saturn goes into Sagittarius, you will have knowledge to take around the world. It will then be the time for the teacher and the healer to work together. Be careful not to get caught up in self-righteousness or any extreme love-hate situations. Saturn will take them right into your body and you will feel dis-ease.

Uranus Transiting Ophiuchus

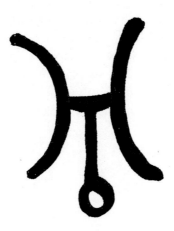

Glyph: Derivation of the letter "H" for its discover Sir William Herschel, in 1781
Transiting Time: About five years
Appearance: Approximately every 84 years
Keywords: Sudden awakenings
Key Phrase: Flashes of great insight into the unknown
Association with The Body and Mind: Circulatory system, paralysis, cramps, sudden nervous breakdowns, physical changes, the Third Eye and the Subtle Body

When Uranus is transiting Ophiuchus, your emotions run high and intense. There is a freeing of spirit; you find it easy to laugh and look at things differently. New ideas come to you. You are fascinated with science and metaphysics, maybe even with UFOs. You will have a natural insight into the paranormal. There's a Merlin quality you can carry—wizard, genius, magical sorcerer—because of sudden flashes of brilliance. Much of your insight will come about in your own body. You will have the ability to access the power to heal. You will intuitively know the best way to take care of the physical and subtle body. Your progressive thinking allows you to embrace new ideas freely and travel through the ether by tapping into the collective unconscious. It will be up to you to decide whether you connect with it or not; the door is open.

As I write this book Uranus is in Aquarius and it may be some time before it reaches Ophiuchus. Do check what aspects are being made to Uranus from other planets transiting Ophiuchus and blend in this information. For example, the moon journeys through Ophiuchus once a month and makes many different aspects to Uranus in its travels. Astrology is about blending. Just as painting is about blending colors and making different shades. Astrology is about layering all the different aspects and mixing them into an alchemic blend.

Neptune Transiting Ophiuchus

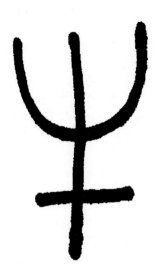

Glyph: The god of the sea, trident of Poseidon
Transiting Time: About Seven Years
Appearance: Approximately every 165 years
Keywords: Powerful Intuition
Key Phrase: Psychic Knowingness
Association with The Body and Mind: Spinal cord, mental and nervous process, the thalamus, pineal gland, the Third Eye and the Subtle Body

Neptune transiting Ophiuchus gives you prophetic dreams, a need for a deeper understanding of life. You travel in your dreams to unknown lands and bring back information. It is as if you are on the Internet and are able to tap into your unconscious or that all-knowing part of the brain. You can be very philosophical and love to explore the powers of the mind. You have great regenerative power to heal. You escape into your art, which can be painting, poetry, writing, photography, or the healing arts. You easily understand the body and you can detect any dis-ease in it. Your Third Eye is wide open.

People born when Neptune is in Ophiuchus are more evolved than others and are always searching for the truth. Most of the time they are open enough to receive it. For the natural state of the universe is abundance; we are the ones that keep us from receiving what is rightfully ours.

(Note: It may be a long time before Neptune transits Ophiuchus, but Neptune will be making aspects between different planets transiting Ophiuchus that can hit off this energy.)

Chiron Transiting Ophiuchus

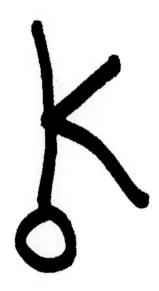

Glyph: Discovered by astronomer Charles Kowall of the Hale Observatory on November 1, 1977
Transiting Time: About 2 years and 14 days
Appearance: Approximately once every 50 years
Keyword: Initiation
Key Phrase: The Wounded Healer
Association with The Body and Mind: All of the parts that need to be healed as well as the subtle body

As Chiron travels through the different signs in the Zodiac, it heals that part of you which is represented by that sign. It is called the healing journey as it moves around the Zodiac. What is Chiron healing in Ophiuchus? It's healing the healer. It is exposing each and every one of us to the ability to heal ourselves. You will seek to transform yourself in order to overcome your ego: the ego that keeps you separated by believing that what you do and how you feel doesn't affect everyone on this planet, the ego that keeps you in the survival mode and not understanding that we are all one. With Chiron in Ophiuchus, you will have some encounters with death and will experience a rebirth. Then you will be able to feel more alive in your own life.

As a healer, you will be able to reach people who are trapped in the pain of darkness and despair. With your knowledge and experience, you now have the ability to shine light into their darkness. Chiron in Ophiuchus makes us aware—often painfully.

> *Much of your pain is self-chosen.*
> *It is the bitter potion by which the*
> *Physician within you heals your sick self*
> *Therefore trust the physician, and drink*
> *His remedy in silence and tranquility:*
> *For his hand, though heavy and hard, is*
> *Guided by the tender hand of the Unseen*

—Kahlil Gibran,

In other words, when dis-ease is in your body, your realized self or your god self is just telling you that you must change what you are doing or your body is going to shut down. The question you must ask yourself is "Where am I not loving?" When you can answer that question, you will know the reason of your dis-ease. Most of the time, this is easier said than done.

Pluto Transiting Ophiuchus

Glyph: Pluto has two different glyphs. One comes from "PL" for its discoverer, Percival Lowell in 1930. The other represents the cross of matter topped by the crescent moon and hovers above the circle of infinity.

Transiting Time: Very erratic, eight to 13 years

Appearance: Roughly every 285 years

Keywords: Transformation

Key Phrase: Destroying then recreating

Associations with The Body and Mind: Creative and regenerative forces of the body, the gonads, glands that produce, reproductive cells, the unconscious, enforced changes, eruption, beginnings and ends of phases of life, The Third Eye and The Subtle Body.

Pluto exposes all that is hidden, uncovers all that is secret. Pluto represents that which is born, that which dies, and that which is born again. You can relate it to Shiva, the Hindu god of transformation. Shiva, like Pluto, represents the complete cyclical process of generation, destruction and regeneration. Pluto's actions are slow, but the slow planets are the ones that affect you the most. It takes a while for his presence to be felt, but when it is, you will be completely transformed. Whatever Pluto touches never remains the same. Pluto is the transformer, he is the rebel of the solar system. If you fight the change, Pluto will take you to your knees, where you will remain until you do change.

Pluto is currently activating Ophiuchus, the healer, and the doctor. Guess what's going to change? Your whole understanding about sickness and healing, why you get sick, and how to heal yourself. The word Pluto literally means riches and treasures. Pluto is giving us the gift of activating Ophiuchus. Through this activation, he is giving you the power to understand what your body is about as well as how to heal it and listen to

125

it. You will also know that you have two bodies - the physical body and the subtle body. The subtle body is where the healing begins.

CHAPTER SIX
New Beginnings

Ordinary reality is only the top layer of our sandwich.
—Deepak Chopra

On November 13, 2012, there will be a total solar eclipse in Ophiuchus. This eclipse is closely tied to the total solar eclipse of August 1999. The 1999 configuration was that of a grand cross. It formed a point in the heavens that is referred to as "The Point of The Avatar." November 13, 2012 is 13 years after the 1999 eclipse. This eclipse will be in alignment with Ophiuchus, the 13th constellation of the Zodiac. This constellation is the archetype of the shaman or healer who has knowledge of the secret of life. In the terms of galactic whole-sky astrology, this eclipse will represent the initiation of our planet into the mysteries that Ophiuchus represents.

The 13-year period following the 1999 activation is and will continue to be a time of profound change. With the help and awareness of Ophiuchus and the tools he has made available to us, we will be able to integrate these new galactic energies. In the 13th year after the 1999 activation, there will be a series of three major astronomical events in rapid succession. If we have been working with the energy Ophiuchus brought in, we will do fine.

The first of these events will be November 13, 2012—the total eclipse. The second will be the winter solstice - which is the final solstice in the galactic plane alignment series. The third event will be on December 31, 2012 when Sirius aligns with our planet and the Sun at midnight. Some say, and I believe, that we may be from Sirius. Others say we have a destiny with Sirius. It is interesting to note that we are moving through space with Sirius B in a spiral that is identical to the heliacal plane of the DNA molecule.

Let me put it this way: Ophiuchus has been offering us new concepts in healing, rejuvenation techniques, awareness activation and raising the body's vibration. With total eclipse in Ophiuchus, November 2012, planet Earth will achieve a higher frequency with a whole new formula for body health, harmony and spirituality.

The Universe is not only stranger then we imagine, but stranger than we can imagine.

Your Sun Sign Ophiuchus
November 30 to December 17

My Dear old Sagittarius, look at you now; and for those born after 1995, you are our Ophiuchians.

What lies before us and what lies behind us
Are small matters compared to
What lies within us.
And when we bring what is within
Out into the world,
Miracles happen
—Henry David Thoreau

Thoreau must have been thinking of you, my dear Ophiuchians. You will go to extremes and travel far and wide to find the answer to the age-old question, "What is the meaning of life?" You know that you can pull just about any information that you want from the ethers around you. You have this uncanny ability to be able to tap into the source (the collective unconscious), yet that is not good enough. It's too easy; you reject much of the knowledge that comes to you effortlessly. Off you go on your freedom-loving, overindulging, push-to-the-limit jaunts. As you age, you will acknowledge that the knowledge you are seeking is found from within and all that globetrotting was just for fun.

Many of your dreams are prophetic; you can see the bigger picture, and then you love to philosophize about it. You have an incredible thirst for knowledge but find it hard to be tied to a classroom. You love the outdoors, being with nature, and meeting people in foreign places. You believe they will have the answers, and you have a hard time accepting the fact that your power and all the answers are already inside you. This all changes with age. At the same time, you do know that the power of laughter can heal. Ophiuchians have a delicate ability to heal the people around them. Sometimes this power will frighten you. Still, you feel that

128

you have a well of limitless energy, and you crave any opportunity to try something new.

You've known the power of positive thinking and are able to achieve many of your goals. Help always comes to you from out of the ethers, and sometimes you are very idealistic.

Yours is the most powerful sign of the Zodiac - you have not even begun to become your realized self. You have spent most of your life running from what you know to be true. Even if you are fifty years old in the year 2000, your sun sign has only been activated for about five years, so the energy surrounding it is still young, yet growing fast. You know you have the ability to transform yourself and others. You have a tremendous emotional force behind your actions. You also have a highly secretive part of yourself. It is buried so deep inside that you are afraid of what it would bring forward if your light were to shine on it. As you become more Ophiuchan, you know that this was one of the things that had to come into fruition, knowing that you were different all the while.

Now, as your fears begin to vanish, you are able to free yourself in order to investigate the unknown, the underworld, and the fourth dimension. As you are quickly developing spiritually, you will derive immense power from your ability to tap into the first harmonic creative, regenerative forces of nature. You will be able to draw all the energy you need from a tree, a flower, a sunset, to rejuvenate and regenerate life. You will be able to heal not only yourself but also others, almost miraculously. You will have no fear of the unknown or of death. You will have a mystical understanding of the cyclical nature of manifestation as you come to realize that all disease, (dis - ease) within you is due to a lack of love somewhere in your life.

You understand that anything less than unconditional love and understanding and forgiveness causes dis-ease in the body, and that can result in sickness. You will come to understand all dis-ease in the body and the light of insight shown upon it will remove and cure anything. Even your beliefs that at a certain age one must get old and die will change. With your sun in Ophiuchus, it is your understanding that what you think, you are, and you prove that to yourself over and over again. As Louise Hay said, "What you believe to be true, you prove to yourself to be true 100 percent of the time."

You will also come to understand that we were all created equal, but not *born* equal because of past lives and karmas. There is no such thing as an accident; things happen because we attract them. If we feel guilty about something, guilt always seeks punishment. We can attract anything from a stubbed toe to a major car accident. All this knowledge will open up wide to you, as you, the Ophiuchan, use your Third Eye.

Some of you are well on your journey, and you will lead this planet into the fourth dimension. Remember, Ophiuchus, you are the physician, the healer. You have come to help raise the consciousness of our species as this beautiful planet evolves and we move into the fourth and fifth dimensions.

Pay more attention to your feelings and forget thinking.
While the mind needs to learn, the body simply knows.
—Don Juan to Carlos Castaneda (1925-1998)

When I asked Ophiuchan, Robert Hand, an internationally famous astrologer and one I have great respect for, "What do you think about Ophiuchus as the 13th sign? And have you written anything on him? Robert Hand's reply was, "Ophiuchus is definitely a 13th zodiacal constellation but signs are not constellations even though they bare the name of constellations. I believe that the constellations should be used along side of the signs and images that have affects. I have not written anything on this yet."

Ophiuchus As Your Rising Sign

The real voyage of discovery consists not
In seeking new landscapes but in having
new eyes.
—Marcel Proust (1871-1922)

The Rising sign is found by the date and time of day you were born, and the time of sunrise that day. The Sun shows our inner personality, the ego, and the animus—or male characteristics that dominate our identity. The Moon is associated with the emotional quality or the anima - the feminine, sensitive side of our instincts. The Rising (ascendant) Sign is our mask. It is what we show the world, our behavior. It deals with the

First House, our physical body. The physical body is a vehicle to carry us through life; the ascendant depicts the kind of vehicle we have chosen.

The rising sign also describes the psychological device we use to keep our true self safe. It is connected to our survival instincts and protects our real identity, which is our sun sign. The ascendant is likened to a butterfly in its cocoon. We have to grow into our sun sign, and sometimes that takes a lifetime.

Ophiuchus—the opener of the Third Eye- helps us evolve. This mask that you use, your ascendant, is crystal clear and works as a magnifying glass now into yourself. This is a very powerful sign, and it will take time to learn to work with the energies Ophiuchus brings with him. These energies are strong, and loving, and you will grow with them. You may have gone through great pain and turbulence, both emotionally and physically. As the physician, you must first heal yourself.

> To heal your world,
> You must first heal yourself.
> To heal yourself
> You must first see the source of your dis-ease.
> To see the source,
> You must see your inner self.
> To see your inner self,
> You must be willing to let go.
> To let go is to breathe
> To breathe in the ethers of Ophiuchus.

If this is now your new rising sign, it may explain all the difficulties you have endured, especially in the last five years. Sometimes, in order to be a good teacher and healer, you may have to experience disappointment or loss. There are a few evolved souls who know and understand this without having experienced it. If you're in pain, (of any kind) practice the subtle body and third eye exercises and be one of the few who understand that physical or mental agony is a tool to get us back on track, to becoming our realized selves.

Some say there is no scientific proof that astrology really works. That's a good reason for astrology to be a bit more scientific and exacting. Astrology is called an art because it is part science and part intuition. My intuition shouts loudly to me and says; use Ophiuchus. My art, my sense of balance and beauty tells to me it's time for Ophiuchus. The scientific part of me says, "How can you not use Ophiuchus?" Again, I stress that astrology can not operate in a vacuum. The people of the planet Earth really want to believe in astrology. It's been around longer than any religion, and it can be traced back to pre-history.

CHAPTER SEVEN
By Their Symbols Shall Ye Know Them

If the laws of nature were deeply explored,
we would one day know the mind of God.
—Stephen Hawking

Ophiuchus is the 13th sign of the Zodiac. The number 13 has a great deal of symbolism that relates to the sign itself. It is a number of radical change. The best way I can explain the number 13 is by using the metaphor of the butterfly. We lived in the garden as caterpillars, and for the last 3,500 years we have been living in a cocoon. Now we are ready to emerge from this cocoon to transform into a beautiful butterfly. We are ready to fly above to a separate reality as we wake up to the knowledge that Ophiuchus is bringing. We are about to use more of our brains and understand that we are the people of the earth and that we are one. We will wake up to the fact that we will invent and find a way to travel to other galaxies as soon as we know we are one people of the earth with one godhead. As long as we stay separated from one another, we can't travel to other galaxies.

Numerology And The Number 13

He who understands the number 13 will be
given power and dominion—The Ancients

Numerology is the study of numbers and their meanings. Its beginnings were much like those of astrology. Most of the early teachings were transmitted orally and only to a chosen few, because the information was considered sacred and very powerful. In the sixth century B.C., Pythagoras believed that reality is mathematical and that order is created out of chaos through numbers. This is the principle upon which numerology is based.

Pythagoras' modern-day counterpart is mathematician Albert Einstein, who introduced the theory of relativity. Einstein changed the belief in the absolute, and humanity finally awakened to new ideas and possibilities

133

about our relationships with things that shape our views of life. Science saw the universe as a far greater and more complex place that had previously been thought. The universe is now easier to understand. Symbols and myths only reveal our relationships in this time and space and can change, for life is forever changing and mysterious. In Albert Einstein's essay, *"The World As I See It,* he said, "The most beautiful experience we can have is the mysterious." Now take the mysterious symbolism of the 13th sign, Ophiuchus, as an important change in the Zodiac and interpret both its esoteric and mundane meanings.

In Numerology, the number 13 represents death and rebirth, regeneration and change. Let's break it down as a compound number. Thirteen is death to the old so that the new can be born (the King is dead, long live the King.) The number one in the 13 means new beginnings. The number three in 13 means freedom—freedom to change and to create, to see life from a new perspective. Add the one and the three together, and you get four. Four is balance and manifestation.

Ophiuchus as the 13th sign is bringing us:

> One - New beginnings 1
> Three - Freedom to create + 3
> Four - Manifestation through balance 4

Numerology is inseparable from astrology. Both are intertwined along with the Tarot, passed down to us by the ancients long before the Egyptians, to be used as tools to help us understand and guide our passage through the Valley of the Shadows.

Illustrations from the Universal Waite, Medieval Scapini and Hanson-Roberts Tarot decks reproduced by permission of U.S. Games Systems, Inc. Stamford, CT 06902. Copyrights 1990, 1985 and 1985 respectively by U.S. Games Systems, Inc., Stamford, CT. Further reproduction prohibited.

Tarot and the 13th Card

The Tarot is just like astrology and numerology in that we don't know its origin. The Tarot is a deck of 78 cards that can also be used to tell what may happen in the future on the path you are following. It is also to be used as a tool of self-discovery. We can trace the Tarot back to well before the ancient Egyptians. The journey through the Tarot is very much like the journey we travel through the 12 houses of Astrology. The Tarot Cards have numbers on them, and the 13th card is the Death Card. The card with Death—or the words, "La Morte" written on the bottom—is the most misunderstood card in the deck. It is depicted either with a skeleton riding a horse or a skeleton swinging the scythe. Both symbolize movement.

In the Waite Deck (the most widely used), there is a horse that symbolizes power, desire, and the cosmos. The horse is white for purity, openness and light. The red plume on the skeleton's helmet indicates earthly passions. The skeleton is protected with armor as he rides over a prostrate king wearing a crown. The armor is Mars, and the King is man-made power; the crown is sovereignty. The skeleton carries a flag with a white rose on it; the rose symbolizes heavenly perfection. In the flag's background the sun is rising - there is new life and a new day. The Sun symbolizes supreme cosmic power, light, vitalizing energy and life. The river in the background symbolizes movement and the unconscious; floating on the river is a ship symbolizing the transcending of the material plane; it is the ship of life. The color gold represents the divinity and solar principle of energy. To me, this sounds a lot like what Ophiuchus is about.

In the deck of cards with the skeleton and scythe, the 13th card shows the scythe cutting down men in a field of grass. Thirteen is the number representing upheavals. Therefore, new ground may be broken. But if the scythe is used for selfish purposes, it will bring destruction upon itself. The number 13 is also associated with genius, challenging the orthodox with new discoveries. In one sense, the skeleton is impersonal and universal. Yet it is also deeply personal, hidden within ourselves, buried underneath our flesh. We can touch our skin, but under normal circumstances we can't touch our bones. We seldom see our bones, just as we seldom "see" our unconscious, or that part of the brain that is unused. Yet our bones are our truest self. When we are given an x-ray, it is like having insight into the hidden and the unknown. There is a saying among astrologers: The Skeleton is about getting back to the basics, the bare bones of reality.

The Skeleton of card 13 shows us many opposites and contradictions. It can look like bare bones- lifeless—or it can symbolize pure beings. The Skeleton with the scythe and dismembered bodies, which look as though they have been planted in a garden, represents a transformation that divides up and regenerates. It is not an accident that Ophiuchus is the 13th sign.

Some people consider 13 unlucky. Most hotel, apartments and office buildings don't have a 13th floor. The 13 intrudes into the twelve hours of our daytime, and the twelve months of the year. It breaks up the rhythm of our daily lives. There is no room on our calendar, and no spot on our clock, for the number 13.

We experience the intrusion of this skeleton as a betrayal, just as twelve disciples, plus Judas, makes 13. There are 12 signs of the traditional Zodiac; Ophiuchus is the 13th. The coming of the 13th is the dying of the old notion of there being only 12 signs of the Zodiac. Ophiuchus deals with spiritual enlightenment and death. Until we can bring in the 13th sign and evolve above the old limitations of the 12 signs, we will be trapped into accepting our physical mortality. Let Ophiuchus free us from the traditional 12 to rise above with the 13th.

The Reason Why

The fault, dear Brutus, is not in our stars, but in ourselves.
-William Shakespeare

Ophiuchus is in the Zodiac; Ophiuchus is in the ethers; Ophiuchus is here. We experience Ophiuchus' vibration when we transcend ordinary consciousness by channeling our pain into art, writing, composing or anything creative. Ophiuchus, the physician of wholeness is making us aware of the power that dwells within us. Ophiuchus is here to bring home the truth about healing and sickness, and to make it very clear that all sickness is just our bodies delivering this message:

Look what you are creating here.

Our bodies are very finely tuned instruments. In fact, our bodies are the most intricate, sophisticated, sensitive systems on the planet, holding within them all the information we could ever possibly need. If we can retrieve and interpret this information correctly, then we can put it to use. Ophiuchus is here to help us know:

Health is not a condition of the body but of the mind.

Why do so many people readily admit that they can make themselves sick, but are reluctant to acknowledge that they can make themselves well? Everything we think, say and believe, makes an impression on our minds and bodies. What we give out always comes back. As we move more into Ophiuchus' vibration, it comes back almost instantly. It is all about love-nonjudgmental, unconditional love of ourselves and others. Ophiuchus is here to expand our minds, and make us mindful of our bodies and emotions. If we could keenly observe the feelings in our bodies, we could find that the Garden of Eden is right here. Ophiuchus is here, back with the snake and the apple. Eat of the fruit of the tree of knowledge and use it wisely. If we understand that we should stay out of the pain of the past and the fear of the future, we should be able to stay present in our bodies. We will come to know everything and not be separated from the source.

Life is a continuum, always transforming, always dying to the old and being born to the new. We never really die - we just change. Ophiuchus is here to bring home this message, which is not too different from the one Jesus and many other great teachers, healers and prophets gave us.

There is only one religion
The religion of love
There is only one language
The language of the heart
There is only one race
The race of humanity
There is only one God
And he is omnipresent
—*Sai Baba*

EPILOGE
Reflections

I came of age in New York City
where the night skies were of
neon and bright lights reflected
from the pulsating city below,
When I caught a glimpse of a sunset
or the glimmer of the full moon
it was quite a magical moment
for this city girl,
It never occurred to me
to look up at the sky
and see the location of a planet
I had an ephemeris for that
The planetarium
during the late 60's, 70's and 80's
(my tender years as an astrologer)
was a great place for Pink Floyd and
The Grateful Dead Concerts.
Then in the 1990s
it was closed, to be rebuilt
Today it stands awesome
bearing witness to the magnificence of the cosmos
and our ever changing knowledge of
the stars, the planets and

The 13th Sign

I can understand why something so visible, is so invisible ...

ACKNOWLEDGMENTS

Special thanks. To Dr. Marlene Lazar and Valerie Antonik, for helping this dyslexic, by deciphering the words on the page.

And for all the beautiful art in the book:

David Malin
    Photographic scientist-astronomer also known as "The Man who Colors Stars". It is his photograph on the cover of the book, of the area of the sky that Ophiuchus is in. Mr. Malin is associate with the Anglo-Australian Observatory and is based in Sydney, Australia. For more information check out the web page.

Michael Oates
    Manchester Astronomical Society, Godlee Observatory, U.M.I.S.T Sackville Street, Manchester M60 IQD England. For His Atlas Celeste by Jon Bevis (ca 1750)

Linda Hall Library
    Out Of This World, The Golden Age of the Celestial Atlas
    510 Cherry Street, Kansas City, Missouri 64110

Dr Edward Bach
    Dr. Edward Bach Centre, for the Flower Remedies. Mount Vernon, Oxfordshire, England
    Check out the web address for instructions on how to make remedies and also publications, courses,
history and any other information.

Matrix Software
    Astrology software used in this book and over the years. 407 M. State Street, Big Rapids, MI. Check out their web page.

John Walker

Fourmilab, Switzerland. He is the founder of Autodesk, Inc. John's web site gave us the images of the stars and plants at any given time and location.

I would like to acknowledge my Spirit Guides, Angels and Urania. Urania, "the Heavenly," is the muse for astronomy and astrology.

GLOSSARY

Alchemy Transformation or enchanting power, a power especially of enchantment or transformation.

Allopathic The principle of mainstream medical practice, as opposed to that of homeopathy.

Ascendant The First House or Rising Sign. The point at which the eastern horizon intersects the ecliptic. Reflects the personality or outward approach of the individual.

Aspect Angled degrees between two celestial bodies, which form some meaningful combination.

Cardinal Signs The sign of the changing seasons, Aries, Cancer, Libra and Capricorn. They are active, outgoing, and noticeable.

Chakra Energy points in the body. We have seven main chakras. The first chakra is the base chakra located in the base of the spine and is perceived as red. The second chakra is located in the sexual organs, color orange. Third chakra is located in the solar plexus (stomach area), color yellow. The fourth chakra is the heart chakra, color green. The fifth chakra is the throat chakra, color blue. The sixth chakra located in the center of the forehead - Third Eye, color indigo. The seventh or crown chakra is located on the top of the head and is white.

Chart The 12 signs, 12 houses, 360 degree zodiac, one's individual horoscope draft.

Chi, Ch'i Chinese philosophy, the energy or life force of the universe, believed to flow around the body and to be present in all living things

Conjunction The occurrence of a direct or nearly direct lineup of planets, in nearly same orb or degree with each other.

143

Consciousness There are seven levels of consciousness:

1. Low level of Consciousness, this intelligence directs and coordinates the life functions; we are alive but unconscious.
2. Subliminal Level Consciousness. We are alive but we are in a dream state.
3. Consciousness, this is what we are living in right now with leaky borders into the fourth.
4. The field of Consciousness when we are aware of what we attract to us, aware of all our actions, the ability to increase synchronicity in the events in our lives.
5. Consciousness of clairvoyancy, to see clearly with the Third Eye.
6. The Higher Self consciousness, the ability to tap into the Collective Unconscious to know everything.
7. Realized-self, Christ-self in this level consciousness; we can create anything at will, instantaneously.

Cusp – The beginning of a house position in the chart.

Dimension Similar, but not the same as the seven levels of consciousness. There are seven dimensions:

☐ *First dimension.* Supports plant life.
☐ *Second Dimension.* Animal and human life. You can find a near perfect representation of two-dimensional man, the simple peasant man in Don Quixote.
☐ *Third Dimension.* The creative human. Most of us are working this level. You can make things happen if you put forth effort. For example, if you want a candy bar you need to know where to get one and have the money to buy it. (Hamlet in Shakespeare is a third-dimensional man)
☐ *Fourth Dimension.* The awareness of working with energies of synchronicity; a candy bar shows up.
☐ *Fifth Dimension.* Knowing human working with the higher self; you can materialize the candy bar. Merlin qualities
☐ *Sixth Dimension.* Christ energy. Buddha
☐ *Seventh Dimension.* God. Omnipresent

Degree There are 360 degrees in a chart; Zodiac longitudes.

Eclipse A Solar eclipse occurs when the Moon is between the Sun and Earth, cutting off the light of the Sun from Earth. A Lunar eclipse occurs when the Earth is between the Moon and the Sun, cutting off the light of the Sun from the moon.

Ecliptic The path the Earth orbits the Sun extended into space to meet the celestial sphere.

Elements Each sign in the Zodiac is grouped into certain common characteristics and personality traits of the sign: Fire (fiery), Earth (earthy), Air (sociable), Water (deep) and Ether (messenger).

Ephemeris Book or almanac listing the planets' places for any time. The oldest almanac is in the British Museum and dates 1431. It's said Columbus navigated by the aid of an Astrologer's Ephemeris.

Ether The sky or the upper reaches of the atmosphere and outer space that carry energy waves.

Fixed Signs Taurus, Leo, Scorpio, Aquarius; they are determined, unyielding.

Flower Essences Like other forms of homeopathic medicine, these take effect by treating the individual, not the dis-ease or symptoms of disease. They work specifically on the emotional condition to cure the problem, the dis-ease. That then cures the physical body.

Glyph A symbol used to denote a sign of the zodiac or planet.

Horoscope A chart or map of the position of the planets in the heavens at the exact time and place of one's birth.

House One of 12 divisions made in the astrology chart. Each house is associated both with a different aspect of one's life and with a specific zodiac sign. Except for the 8th house that now has two zodiac signs, Ophiuchus and Scorpio.

Kundalini Vital energy heat which Hindus believe lies dormant at the base of the spine until it is called into action; e.g. through yoga, to be used in seeking enlightenment.

Latitude Angular distance of a specific point on the Earth's surface from the Earth's equator.

Mode Based on the astrological sign's function and personality. There are four modes for 13 signs in the Zodiac: Intuition, Feeling, Sensation, and Thought.

Muse In Greek mythology, nine daughters of Zeus. The Muses inspired and presided over the different creative arts. Urania is the muse for astronomy.

Mutable Signs Gemini, Virgo, Sagittarius and Pisces. They are adaptable, versatile and they blend.

Natal Chart Horoscope, drawn from the moment of birth showing the location of planets at that time.

New Age The Age of Aquarius

Opposition When planets are in opposing houses. At 180-degree angle or aspects from each other. Two planets directly across from each other in the horoscope chart.

Ophiuchus The 13th sign of the Zodiac

Planets There are 12 planets when working with astrology: Earth, Mars, Venus, Mercury, Jupiter, Saturn, Uranus, Neptune, Pluto, also includes the Sun, the Moon and Chiron.

Pluto Planet that represents total transformation, death and rebirth; rules Scorpio and Ophiuchus, Ruler of the Eighth house.

Prana Sanskrit for, the breath of life, the life force, breathing. Breath control used in yoga for self-awareness.

Precession The precession of the equinoxes that take the constellations through all the 13 Zodiac Signs in about 26,000 years in apparent backward motion through the zodiac. It takes about 2,000 years for the earth to travel through each sign. We are now in the Aquarian Age as of 2000A.D. leaving the Piscine Age, from 0-2000 A.D.

Progression Astrologers use the formula of one day for each year to advance the natal chart.

Qualities The 13 signs of the zodiac are divided into three groups: Cardinal (initiatory), Fixed (determined), and Mutable (versatile).

Retrograde The apparent backward motion of the planets. For example, when the planet Mercury (the messenger) goes retrograde, there are problems with communications. All planets go retrograde at different times, except the sun and the moon.

Rising Sign Same as Ascendant; see ascendant.

Royal Astronomical Society Founded in 1820 in London, England. The Society's aims are the encouragement and promotions of astronomy and geophysics. Its main functions are to publish the results of astronomical and geophysical research as well as to maintain as complete a library as possible in these subjects.

Ruler Planets are said to rule certain signs. For example, Aries is ruled by Mars, the Greek god of war. Venus, the goddess of love, rules Taurus

Sai Baba Bhagavan Sri Sathys Sai Baba. To millions over the entire world, Saia Baba is believed to be an Avatar, an embodiment of God, divinity in human form. He is from India.

Sextile A favorable 60-degree aspect between planets.

Shadow Side Jungian archetype that represents aggressive and sexual instincts inherited from primitive stage of humanity. We all have both a shadow side (hidden) and a light side (apparent.)

147

Subtle Body Sometimes referred to as our Astral Body or over body. When it is perceived clairvoyantly, it looks similar to our physical body.

Synchronicity A non-causal connecting principle, linking seemingly unrelated events. Term was first used by Carl Jung.

Third Eye Located in the center of the forehead, the eye in which we perceive things.

Transit The actual passage of a planet through the individual horoscope, having a special impact as it aspects natal house and other planets.

Trine The most favorable aspect, representing an angular relationship of 120 degrees.

Urania The muse for Astrology and astronomy (which helped oversee this book).

Zodiac An imaginary band across the heavens; the 13 signs of the horoscope as they form a 360-degree circle.

NOTES

NOTES

NOTES

BIBLIOGRAPHY & SUGGESTED READING

Over the years of studying astrology I have come across many great books. Some I committed to memory. Some I used so much that I actually wore them out. These books include:

Arroyo, Stephen. *Astrology Karma & Transformation.* Reno, NV: CRCS Publications,1978

Adrienne, Carol. *The Numerology Kit.* New York, NY: New American Library, 1988

Astronomy. America's Best-Selling Astronomy Magazine. Waukesha, WI: Kalmbach Publishing

Avery, Jeanne. *The Rising Sun.* New York, NY: Doubleday, 1982

Bach, Dr. Edward. *The Back Flower Remedies.* New Canaan, CT: Keats Publishing, 1997

Blavatsky, H.P. *The Secret Doctrine.* Wheaton, IL:. Quest Books, 1971

Brady, Linda, and Evan St. Lifer. *Discovering Your Soul Mission.* New York, NY: Random House, 1998

Buess, Lynn. *Numerology for the New Age.* Sedona, AZ: Light Technology, 1978

Camilleri, Stephanie. *The House Book.* St. Paul, MN: Llewellyn Publications, 1999

Cayce. Edgar. "The Complete Edgar Cayce Readings on CD-Rom." Virginia Beach, VA: Association for Research and Enlightenment, A.R.E. Press, 1999.

Chaney, Robert. *Akashic Records.* Upland, CA: Astara, 1996

Chartrand III, Mark R. *Sky Guide.* New York, NY: Golden Press, 1982

Chopra, Deepak. *Quantum Healing. Ageless Body. Timeless Mind. How to know God* New York, NY: Random House 2000

Clow, Barbara Hand. *Chiron.* St. Paul, MN: Llewellyn Publications, 1987

Cornelius, Geoffrey and Paul Devereux. *The Secret Language of the Stars and Planets.* San Francisco, CA: 1996

Davis, Dylan Warren. *Astrology and Health.* London, England: Headway, Hodder & Stoughton, 1998.

Dodge, Ellin. *Numerology.* New York, NY: Simon & Schuster, 1988

Edelstein, Emma J. & Ludwig. *Asclepius, Collection and Interpretation of Testimonies.* Baltimore, MD, and London, England: The John Hopkins University Press, 1945

Ekrutt, Joachim. *Stars and Planets.* Barron's Nature Guide, Barron's

Encarta. *World English Dictionary.* New York, NY: Bloomsbury Book. St Martin's Press (Microsoft) 1999

Fletcher, Jefferson Butler. *Dante.* Notre Dame, IN: The University of Notre Dame, 1965

Frissell, Bob. *Nothing In This Book Is True, But It's Exactly How Things Are.* Berkeley, CA:. 1994

Graves, Robert. *The Greek Myths, Vols. 1 & 2.* New York, NY: Penguin, 1960

Goodman, Linda. *Star Signs and Sun Signs.* New York, NY: St. Martin's Press, 1987

Green, Jeff. *Pluto The Evolutionary Journey of the Soul.* St. Paul, MN, Llewellyn Publications 1985

Hasbrouch, Muriel Bruce. *Tarot and Astrology.* Rochester, VT: Destiny Books, 1941

Jafee, Aniela. *Memories, Dreams, Reflections C.G. Jung.* New York, NY: Random House 1989

Javane, Faith. *Master Numbers.* Atglen, PA: Whitford Press, 1988

Jouanna, Jacques. *Hippocrates.* Baltimore, MD and London, England: The John Hopkins Press Ltd., 1999

Hall, Calvin S., and Vernon J. Nordby. *A Primer of Jungian Psychology.* New York, NY: Penguin, 1973

Hand, Robert. *Planets in Transit.* Atglen, PA. Whiteford Press 1976

Hay, Louise L. *You Can Heal Your Life.* Carlsbad, CA: Hay House, Inc., 1984

Houston, Jean. *Jump Time.* New York, NY: Penguin Putnam, 2000

Johnson, Robert A. *Transformation. He. She. Owning Your Own Shadow.* San Francisco, CA:. Harper,1991

Llewellyn. *Daily Planetary Guide.* St. Paul, MN: Llewellyn Publications

Lowary, Sheila Petersen. *The Fifth Dimension.* New York, NY: Simon & Schuster, 1988

Maclaine, Shirley. *Going Within.* New York, NY: Bantam Books, 1989

Mann, A. T. *The Round Art: The Astrology of Time and Space.* New York, NY: W.H. Smith Publishers, 1979

March, Marion D. and Joan McEvers. *The Only Way To Learn Astrology* (Vols. 1-6). San Diego, CA:. Astro-Analystic Publications and ACS Publications, 1976 and 1981

Millon, Rene. *Teotihuacan: The Place Where Time Began.* London, England: Thames & Hudson, 1993

Muktananda, Swami. *Where Are You Going.* South Fallsburg, NY: SYDA Foundation, 1981

Negua, Joan. *Basic Astrology.* San Diego, CA: ACS Publications, 1978

Nichols, Sallie. *Jung and Tarot.* York Beach, ME: Samuel Weiser, Inc., 1980

O'Brien, Tim. *Light Years Ago.* New York, NY: Black Cat Press, 1992

Parker, Derek & Julia. *The New Compleat Astrologer.* New York, NY: Crescent Books, 1971

Paterson, Helena. *The Handbook of Celtic Astrology.* St. Paul, MN: Llewellyn Publications, 1998

Reinhart, Melanie. *Chiron and The Healing Journey.* New York, NY: Penguin Books, 1989

Rudhyar, Dane. *An Astrological Mandala.* New York, NY: Random House, 1973

Sakoian, Frances, and Louis A. Acker. *The Astrologer's Handbook.* New York, NY: Harper & Row, 1973

Scapini, Luigi. *The Medieval Scapini Tarot.* Stamford, CT: U.S. Games Systems, Inc., 1985

Schulman, Martin. *Karmic Astrology* (In a Series of Four). York Beach, ME: Samuel Weiser, 1978

Stern, Jess. *A Time for Astrology*. New York, NY: Signet, 1972

Stewart, Daniel Blair. Tesla, The Modern Sorcerer. Berkeley, CA Frog, Ltd.1999

Temple, Robert K.G. *The Sirius Mystery*. London, England:. Destiny Books, 1998

Townley, John. *Astrological Life Cycles*. Rochester, VT: Destiny Books, 1980

Universal-Waite. Tarot Cards, Stamford, CT: U.S. Games System, 1980

Mary Francis Abbamonte

WEB SITES FOR FREE HOROSCOPES CHARTS

Below are my favorite "astrology" web sites:

Astro.Com	Liz Green and Robert Hand
StarIQ.Com	Jeff Green, Rick Levine and others
Astrologysoftware. Com	Matrix Software, I use
MountainAstrologer.Com	A great monthly magazine as well

My favorite "Astronomy" web sites:

fourmilab.ch	Virtual Telescope Aim point RA: Fourmilab, Switzerland
aao.gov	Anglo Australian Observatory (David Malin photo on cover)
astronomy.com	Also of magazine, Astronomy
ras.org.uk	The Royal Astronomical Society, London England
u-net.com/ph/mas	The Manchester Astronocal Society

My favorite "Miscellaneous" web sites

Science.nasn.gov	NASA Science News
patheon.org/mythica.html	Mythology
SpaceArt.com	Space Art
bachcentre.com	Flowwer remedies
Lindahall.org	Celesial Atlas at the Linda Hall Lobrary

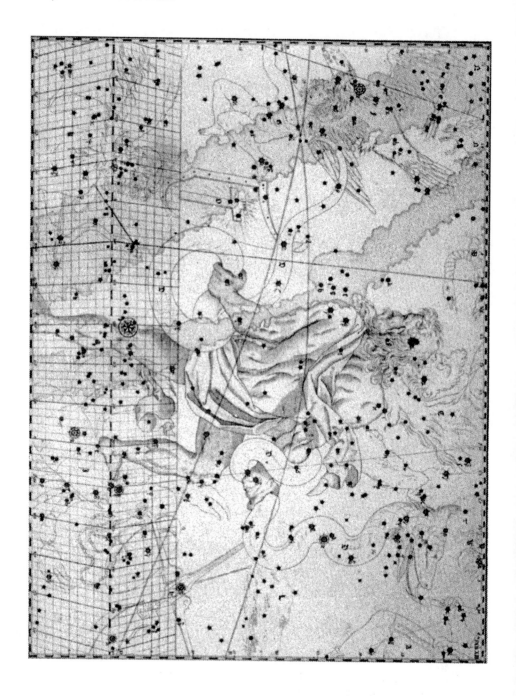

Index

ABOUT THE AUTHOR

Mary Francis Abbamonte believes that a good astrologer needs to tap into their own intuitiveness as well as knowing how to blend all the different aspects. Part of this book is channeled and supported by research. Mary Francis is an intuitive consultant working with astrology, tarot, and numerology since the 1960s. She has a private practice, teaches, and gives workshops in the New York metropolitan area. Mary is a member of The International Society for Astrological Research and The American Federation of Astrologers.

Printed in the United States
40134LVS00005B/208-249